GHOSTS OF THE
SOUTHCOAST

GHOSTS OF THE SOUTHCOAST

TIM WEISBERG

FOREWORD BY JEFF BELANGER, EPILOGUE BY CHRISTOPHER BALZANO

Haunted
America

Published by The History Press
Charleston, SC 29403
www.historypress.net

Back cover image of Lizzie Borden. *Courtesy of Stefani Koorey and Pear Tree Press.*
Unless otherwise stated, all photos are by the author or from the author's collection.

First published 2010

Manufactured in the United States

ISBN 978.59629.142.3

Library of Congress Cataloging-in-Publication Data

Weisberg, Tim.
Ghosts of the SouthCoast / Tim Weisberg.
p. cm.
Includes bibliographical references (p.   ).
ISBN 978-1-59629-142-3
1. Ghosts--Massachusetts--New Bedford Region. I. Title.
BF1472.U6W445 2010
133.109744'8--dc22
2010034446

To my son, Adam, who always asks questions; and to my wife, Jennifer, who always puts up with mine.

CONTENTS

CONTENTS

FOREWORD

"Spooktacular," as Tim Weisberg is so fond of saying on his *Spooky Southcoast* radio show. It's a great word, and it sums up the adventure that is paranormal investigating. If you don't get excited by legends, if you're not exhilarated by the thought of putting yourself into haunted places and seeking out the unknown, then put this book down right now. But, if like many millions of other people all over the world you do suspect there's more to the universe than what we see, keep reading. Your journey into the supernatural side of the SouthCoast begins here.

I'm a person who is passionate about the pursuit of the paranormal. Though I've been in many of the right places for unexplained activity all over the world, I'm usually there at the wrong time. I've had only a handful of experiences that I would truly call paranormal. One of those encounters occurred in the SouthCoast region at the Lizzie Borden House in Fall River, and Tim Weisberg was there when it happened. You'll read more about the Borden history and case later in this book, so I'll stick to what we experienced.

This legend trip was a dream come true for paranormal guys like myself, Tim, Chris Balzano and Matt Moniz. The four of us were alone in the Lizzie Borden house for the evening and had the chance to investigate without anyone else contaminating the environment. It was around 11:30 at night and the four of us were in the basement, just a few feet from the bottom of the stairs. We were quiet, setting up a video camera, and suddenly we heard scampering footsteps and muffled voices right above us in the side hallway leading to the kitchen. Our heads snapped toward each other, our eyes widened—but no one was thinking about ghosts.

We raced up the stairs to the side hallway. No more than four or five seconds had passed between the time we heard the noise and the time we reached the location. We looked around frantically. *No one was thinking ghosts.* We were thinking some kids from Fall River had just broken in and we're in charge for the night. We were not thinking ghosts; we were thinking we needed to call the police; we were thinking we needed to manhandle the intruders out right away—we were *not* thinking ghosts.

I walked over and checked the door. It was locked and secure. Matt looked around the kitchen. Chris and Tim were also looking around the house to see if we missed anything. Nothing. Silence. The four of us looked at each other again. *Whoa* was the consensus. We agreed that it sounded like two sets of feet and the voices sounded like kids. But there was no one there but us. *Now* we were thinking ghosts. If not ghosts, I can't possibly tell you what made those distinct sounds that all of us heard and reacted to.

Ghosts and the paranormal are everywhere. With such a rich history and diverse population, the SouthCoast of Massachusetts is full of these legends. I can think of no better tour guide to show you this stuff than Tim Weisberg. Through reading this book, you're embarking on a supernatural adventure. But don't let it end here. Use this book as a jumping-off point. Get into the field and experience these places and stories for yourself. Legend trip wherever you go, because through the experience you become part of the story that is the SouthCoast.

Jeff Belanger
Author of *Weird Massachusetts*, founder of Ghostvillage.com and host of *30 Odd Minutes*.

ACKNOWLEDGEMENTS

Big thanks go out to Christopher Balzano and Jeff Belanger, who convinced me I could chronicle the ghosts of the SouthCoast and helped me to do so; to my *Spooky Southcoast* cohosts Matt Costa and Matt Moniz, for being at my side while investigating and talking about the subject these past few years; to my friends and family, not only for supporting me when I started talking about ghosts but for also doing the same; to teams and investigators such as Luann Joly and Whaling City Ghosts, Eric LaVoie and Dartmouth Anomalies Research Team, Keith Johnson and New England Anomalies Research, Andrew Lake and Greenville Paranormal Research, Linda Lynch of Veils Edge Paranormal, Loren Coleman, Thomas D'Agostino, Chris Pittman, Mike Markowicz, Carlston Wood, Bob Ethier and a whole community of others to whom I have been privileged enough to work with and learn from; to Stefani Koorey, Ph.D., and Pear Tree Press for the photos; and finally to our radio listeners and the people of the region who have reported their experiences and helped make the SouthCoast just a little bit spookier.

INTRODUCTION

From the time the early British colonists began migrating westward from Plymouth Colony in the 1630s, they knew there was something unusual about the area that would eventually come to be known as the SouthCoast of Massachusetts.

The Native Americans spoke of a special power that existed, and that power still has its hold on the region today. From those original inhabitants to the English of the 1600s to the Portuguese and numerous other cultures of today—through war and through civilization—the ghosts of the SouthCoast have had a direct effect on the land and its people.

And they've been around since the very beginning.

The first Englishman to visit the area—at least that we know of—was Bartholomew Gosnold, often referred to as History's Forgotten Man. After the failure of Roanoke in Virginia and other attempted English settlements in the New World, Gosnold set sail in 1602 aboard the *Concord*, first arriving in Maine and making his way down to Provincetown. There, he gave Cape Cod its name for the fish he observed so abundant in its waters and later named the island of Martha's Vineyard for his daughter, who died in infancy.

Gosnold also explored the Elizabeth Islands off the coast of Cape Cod, and while out on one excursion to Penikese Island, they encountered four Wampanoags in a canoe. When the Native Americans ran off at the sight of the British explorers, Gosnold took their canoe as a prize for England. Perhaps this affront is why, to this very day, the specter of Gosnold's ship, the

Concord, can still be spotted off the shores of the islands and even into the SouthCoast region along its chilly waters.

This can be considered America's earliest ghost story, and in the more than four hundred years since, the legends and lore that have sprung up from this particular area have not only given its residents chills and thrills but also became a deeply rooted part of their culture as well.

From the forts and taverns of the Revolution to the gothic libraries and schools of the Victorian era, so many SouthCoast spots are just as well-known for their haunts as they are their history.

As we examine the ghosts of the SouthCoast, understand that just because you might eventually leave them behind, they may not be ready to leave you. These are powerful, endearing haunts that you'll find are more than just a good campfire story. Those associated with the SouthCoast can always expect its specter to loom over them. Even poor Gosnold, whose brief visit forever changed the lands he claimed for the English crown, met an unexplained end. In 2002, a grave was discovered just outside of Jamestown, Virginia. The remains appeared to be of a man around five-foot-three who died when he was between thirty and thirty-six years of age. There was no indication of how he died or who he was—just a captain's staff. Thorough research has led historians to belief they are the remains of Captain Gosnold, proof that while his body may have been found in Virginia, his ghost—and many, many others—belongs to the SouthCoast.

CHAPTER 1

THE WHAT

A PARANORMAL PRIMER

Before we delve into the ghostly history of the SouthCoast, it's important we understand a bit more about the idea of what exactly we're talking about. The term paranormal means something that is alongside (para, as in parallel) the normal but doesn't fall under what is currently described as normal. That definition recognizes that something considered paranormal may in fact be normal, but that we just don't understand it enough to include it in that category just yet. It differs from the supernatural, which by definition can only exceed the natural and not be inclusive within it.

The hope is that someday, through research and field investigation, we'll be able to figure out exactly why the paranormal occurs, thus bringing it into the realm of the normal. Many, though, think we're not intended to understand it.

Either way, nothing helps sneak a little historical education into our minds like a good ghost story.

GHOSTS

We could list a number of different dictionary and encyclopedic definitions of the word ghost, and while many would come close to explaining the phenomenon, none would be exact.

That's because ghosts have yet to be clearly defined. Mankind has believed in the idea of ghosts for as long as it's understood the concept of mortality;

the understanding of the end of life leads to the desire for something beyond it. Ghosts are referenced in some of our earliest histories, including the Holy Bible and Homer's *Iliad*. Every culture has a word for spirits and many have a strong belief in them.

Through investigation of the paranormal and discussion of the topic on my radio show, *Spooky Southcoast*, I have found my own definition of a ghost to be forever evolving. Is it merely a discarnate soul left to wander in the oblivion that is not quite life and not quite afterlife? Or is its explanation something much more complex, involving quantum mechanics, alternate dimensions and inexplicable time slips?

For my own purposes, I have boiled ghosts down to their very essence— energy. Living human beings are comprised of electrical energy necessary for powering the body's various organs and systems. According to the first law of thermodynamics, energy cannot be created nor destroyed, only changed. That basic scientific law is the tenet on which the concept of a ghost is built. When our physical bodies die, the energy that was used to power them— what some might refer to as the soul—needs to go somewhere. That energy was collected and concentrated within us upon birth, and usually it dissipates back out upon death. However, for reasons not quite understood, sometimes that energy maintains its human form or some element of it. Therefore, the body can still appear completely or partially in the form of an apparition, or the voice can remain reverberating through the air.

At the risk of getting a bit trippy, it's also important to note that such energy doesn't have to actually occupy a human being in order to take the form or essence of one. The living can actually *will* a ghost into existence. Known as "thought forms"—or what the Tibetans referred to as *tulpas*— if enough mental energy is focused, an energetic being can be created. This was proven in the Philip experiments of the early 1970s, in which members of the Toronto Society for Psychical Research wrote a back story for Philip, an English nobleman from the mid-1600s. Although he never actually existed, through focus and many long hours spent around a séance table, his spirit eventually manifested and communicated through knocks and other sounds.

The same exact thing could be the case with a number of the haunts we will examine throughout this book. If a place is old or creepy enough, the legend will inevitably develop that it is haunted. If enough people begin to believe it, it will be—regardless of whether any restless spirits are roaming its grounds. If people are focusing energy into the concept of an entity, that entity can become real.

Of course, all of this is an extremely basic concept of what a ghost might be. I'm not saying it's the correct one, either. So many other variables are eventually brought into the paranormal picture, it's hard to stand hard and fast by any definition of a ghost.

HAUNTINGS

Now that we've got at least some idea of what a ghost is, how is it different from a haunting?

Again, there are a number of definitions for the word haunt, but I prefer to look at it like this: Paranormal activity can occur just about anywhere. But when it is sustained over long periods of time in a specific location, then that location can be considered haunted.

Most paranormal researchers delineate hauntings into one of two categories: either residual or intelligent. A residual haunt is also known as a replay haunt, in which the activity appears to occur over and over, like a section of videotape replaying on a loop. The activity is not interactive and goes through its process oblivious to the living that might surround it. Have you ever heard tales of how if you went to a certain location at a specific time and date—usually the anniversary of some tragedy associated with the spot—you'll be able to see or experience the ghost? It's probably because the activity is residual, an imprint of energy left on that location.

The intelligent haunt is where it gets interesting, especially considering our definition of a ghost as energy that retains its humanistic form. In an intelligent haunt, the entity can and does interact with the living. It might answer questions or respond to certain questions or stimuli. It knows you are there, and it wants to you to know it is there as well. Usually, the best and most convincing evidence of the paranormal comes from an intelligent haunt. But if a ghost is just energy that hasn't dissipated, then how can it continue to retain its consciousness?

That's the million-dollar question of paranormal research, and one that I personally don't think we're any closer to answering than we were when Pliny the Younger recorded his experiences with a phantom in Athens, Greece, in the first century AD.

A PSYCHOLOGICAL IMPRINT

It is also believed that if an event of enough magnitude happens in a certain area, that location can be imprinted by the energies surrounding the event. Have you ever been close to where lightning has just struck? The electricity in the air is palpable, and it lingers for quite some time after the bolt itself has disappeared. The ground where it struck is singed and bears a reminder of what took place.

Often, these haunts are the singed reminders of something that took place long ago in these locations. It can be a happy event or a tragic one, but the end result is the same: a permanent imprint on that particular spot.

FACTORS FOR A HAUNT

If paranormal activity can happen anywhere, why can't it be observed and experienced everywhere? Well, after decades of paranormal research, there are a few factors that are believed to be conducive to a haunt.

Since we're dealing with energy, we need a way for this energy to be contained or recorded in a particular location. Quartz is the second-most abundant mineral in the earth's crust (behind fieldspar) and is a major component of granite, which is prevalent throughout the SouthCoast region and New England as a whole. Take a look at the rocks in your backyard or out in the woods near your home. It's everywhere.

Many of the older locations that are reportedly haunted were built with fieldstone foundations, which would feature a great deal of granite and, subsequently, quartz. Quartz is considered piezoelectric, which means it essentially records and stores energy. That's why it's used in wristwatches, radios and even cellphones. When the right pressure is applied, the energy stored can be released. This is known in some circles as the stone tape theory.

Now that we can trap the energy in a certain spot, we need a way to amplify it. Anywhere with a high level of electrical activity can help with this; some even believe that water, especially rolling water such as a stream or a river can help ionize paranormal activity. It's theorized that when the activity amplifies, there are changes in the electromagnetic field that surrounds it. This is quantified through the use of electromagnetic field (or EMF) detectors. A spike in the EMF of an area might possibly indicate the presence of a spirit.

Also, many who have ghostly encounters often report drafts, chills or cold spots. This is because the ghost attempting to materialize is what's known as an endothermic reaction, in which it draws in energy in the form of heat. The opposite is an exothermic reaction, which usually releases energy in the form of heat. However, it can also release it as energy, light or sound—all three are common forms of paranormal activity.

In my experiences, though, the best amplifier for paranormal activity is a person paying attention to it. By being receptive to the paranormal, it gives it credence and it supplies it with the energy it needs to manifest. Human beings are perhaps the best conductors of the paranormal, even if the debate lingers on about whether we are helping it along or creating it in our own minds.

One must always be careful how much to give it, though. As my good friend and colleague Matt Moniz often quotes from his mentor, Maurice DesJardins: for every step you take toward the paranormal, it takes two toward you.

CHAPTER 2
THE WHY

Before we can examine the haunts of the region, we have to understand the tragic history and the mysteries of the land itself that could be the major factor in why the SouthCoast is so haunted.

Considering our attempted definition of them, no ghost can exist within a vacuum. There has to be something giving power to the paranormal, something that charges the electricity for the spirits to draw upon or opens the doorways for UFOs and mysterious creatures. It's more than just the abundant quartz and bodies of water, the time slips and the thinning membrane between reality and something just beyond it.

John N. Mitchell may have been the disgraced attorney general convicted in the Watergate scandal, but he did provide us with a great quote that applies here: "our attitude toward life determines life's attitude toward us."

That fits perfectly in figuring out just why the SouthCoast and its immediate surroundings are so haunted. In some respects, it's because we've made it that way. Our attitude toward the area has determined its attitude toward us—and we've given it plenty of reasons to not like us too much.

KING PHILIP'S WAR

Even in the history books used in SouthCoast schools, little is taught about King Philip's War.

Often called the Forgotten War, it still stands today as the bloodiest war ever fought on American soil. More of the population died in this war than did the Civil War, and it was a great stain on the young colonies.

Revisionist history likes to look back at the early English colonists as those seeking freedom and opportunity in the New World and the Native Americans of the time as kindly helpers to their cause. Every Thanksgiving, schoolchildren are told the tale of Squanto, the kindly Patuxet who helped the pilgrims get through their first hard winter in Plymouth. What isn't taught is how Squanto, also known as Tisquantum, had been twice kidnapped by English visitors to this land and spent time in Britain before returning to find his people decimated by disease. Because of his close association with the English and his ability to speak their language, the great sachem of the Wampanoag Confederacy of area tribes, Massasoit, used Squanto as an envoy when the permanent settlers arrived in 1620.

However, neither side completely trusted Squanto. Some speculate that his death in 1622 was due to poisoning by fellow members of the Wampanoag Confederacy because he had betrayed his people in favor of the English, who refused to turn over Squanto to the Wampanoags upon such suspicion.

The settlers' early alliance with the Indians was just the beginning of a long period of peace between the English and the Wampanoag tribes that always had the undercurrent of mistrust and dislike that would eventually culminate in war.

The seeds of conflict actually were planted under the guise of peace. Massasoit and the pilgrim leaders forged an early alliance against the neighboring Narragansett tribe. After the Indians helped the pilgrims through their first winter in Plymouth, the two sides signed a peace treaty on March 22, 1621. For more than fifty years, the two sides would stand by each other, even as other tribes such as the Pequots attacked the settlers.

Eventually, more settlers arrived and the Massachusetts Bay Colony was formed. To keep the peace with the English, Massasoit sold them land. To the Indians, it was laughable that the settlers would want to give up anything valuable for something such as land, which they felt no man could rightfully own anyway. The one thing Massasoit wouldn't barter was the beliefs of his people, attempting to stave off the English attempts to convert the Indians to Christianity even as the concept of the Praying Indian began to evolve within neighboring tribes.

In the last years of his life, however, Massasoit saw many of his Wampanoags convert to both the English religion and culture, and the strength of his people diluted over time. His eldest son Wamsutta—whom the English dubbed Alexander—ascended to great sachem upon Massasoit's death, believed to be in either 1661 or 1662. By this time, the colonists and the natives had a completely different relationship than the one Wamsutta's father had fostered with those original pilgrims in Plymouth. The colonists were no longer dependent on the Indians for survival and instead sought to expand their colony deeper into Indian territories. The Indians, no longer able to use furs and other items as trade commodities, could only give up more of their land in exchange for items such as weapons and tools from the English.

As the spread of the English grew and the power of the Indians waned, Wamsutta was desperate to keep his people united. Some historians believe he was suspected of meeting with the Narragansett tribe in order to plan a revolt against the colonists. Others believe he was selling land to opposing colonies instead of the Massachusetts Bay Colony. Either way, Wamsutta drew the suspicions of the colonial governor and was summoned to court at Plymouth, reportedly at gunpoint after he failed to appear under his own free will. At some point in the journey, he fell ill and subsequently died. His brother Metacom—or Philip to the English—became the great sachem after his death.

Metacom had his own suspicions about the mysterious passing of his brother; he felt that someone within the colonial government had poisoned Wamsutta in order to quell a potential rebellion.

With all this ill will beginning to build up between the two sides, it was only a matter of time before something would spark the powder keg. That event came in December of 1674, when Metacom's advisor Wassausmon—known to the English as John Sassamon, one of the Praying Indians—approached Plymouth governor Josiah Winslow to warn him that Metacom was planning to unite with other tribes to attack the settlers. Not long after that, Sassamon's body was found in Assawompset Pond in present-day Lakeville or Middleboro, and the settlers accused Metacom and his warriors of his murder. A fellow Indian named Patuckson claimed to bear witness to three of Metacom's men murdering Sassamon, and the trio became the first to be tried in front of a jury of both whites and Indians. The trio was found guilty and subsequently executed in June of 1675, and the colonists remained convinced that Metacom was somehow involved.

The Wampanoags, however, were not happy with the idea of their people being subjected to the laws and courts of the colonists. As noted by Christopher Balzano is his book *Dark Woods: Cults, Crime and the Paranormal in the Freetown State Forest*:

> *As all of the events of the past few decades—the murder of his brother, the followers leaving by the dozens, and the killing of men found guilty with no evidence—swirled about him, the paranormal stepped in. In an often overlooked nod to the unknown, a total lunar eclipse occurred. The Native Americans in the area saw this as a sign of war and Philip used this to fuel their desire for change.*

A band of Pokanokets soon attacked colonial homes and lay siege to the settlement of Swansea. This ignited what would become known as King Philip's War, even though to this day it is unknown whether those Pokanoket were acting on Metacom's orders.

Winslow led the English and Metacom led an army of Indians that included other tribes as well as his own. Battles raged across New England throughout the rest of 1675 and into 1676, with the Indians first taking the upper hand and then the colonists, with their vast weaponry and resources, eventually battling back. On August 12, 1676, Metacom was captured near Mount Hope in Bristol, Rhode Island, by Captain Benjamin Church and his militia and was shot and killed by John Alderman, a Praying Indian. Alderman kept one of Metacom's hands as a prize, and other body parts were scattered throughout the colony. Legend has it that Metacom's head was staked on a long pole and kept at the entrance to Plymouth for more than twenty years.

The final confrontation of King Philip's War came on August 28, 1676. Church and his men captured the last remaining Wampanoag captain, Anawan, at the rock that now bears his name in modern-day Rehoboth. Even today, Anawan Rock is cited as one of the area's most haunted locations, with reports of phantom fires, phantom drumbeats and a disembodied voice that yells, "*Iootash!*" said to be a Wampanoag phrase meaning "stand and fight."

Anawan's capture signified the end of the war, but its dark history was only beginning to take its grasp on the region.

As we will see, many of the SouthCoast sites associated with King Philip's War are considered haunted by the spirits of those who gave their lives in the conflict. Because of the tragic way in which they met their end, their spirits are forever tied to the spot, their psychological imprint embedded upon it even in these modern times. Most of us have heard tales about homes that are haunted because they're built on an old Indian burial ground. Considering the loss of life endured during King Philip's War, the entire SouthCoast is one big Indian burial ground.

But are the heinous scars of war the reason why this region has so many ghosts lurking in its shadows, or is it possible that King Philip's War itself was just another example of a deeper, darker plague that has loomed over the area since time began?

THE BRIDGEWATER TRIANGLE

Enter the Bridgewater Triangle, a cursed paranormal vortex that is either the direct result of the tumult of King Philip's War or one of the factors that caused it. This area, which covers about two hundred square miles south of Boston and just north of the SouthCoast, has endured reports of just about every kind of paranormal phenomena.

The term Bridgewater Triangle first came into existence in the work of investigator and author Loren Coleman. Known for his work in the field of cryptozoology—the study of hidden or unknown animals, such as Bigfoot— Coleman began referring to the mysterious area as the Bridgewater Triangle in correspondences beginning in the late 1970s. He also wrote about it in a 1980 *Boston Magazine* article, before formally introducing the term to the world in his 1983 classic *Mysterious America*.

At the time, paranormal enthusiasts and followers of the weird knew all about the supposed Bermuda Triangle, the mysterious spot in which many ships and aircraft were said to have disappeared. With all the reports of strange phenomena Coleman was receiving from eastern Massachusetts, he eventually came to realize that much of it was centered on a specific hot spot, and he gave it a catchy name to equate it in people's minds with its Bermudan counterpart. Coleman's original Bridgewater Triangle was much more condensed, but modern reinterpretation of the triangle extends it with the towns of Abington, Freetown and Seekonk as its vertices.

The exact points aren't important, however; further work from Coleman and researchers such as Chris Pittman and Christopher Balzano has shown that the triangle is gradually extending beyond any preconceived borders and the heightened amount of paranormal activity extends to the SouthCoast and beyond into northeastern Rhode Island.

Balzano has also noted that the triangle area has unusually high rates for both crime and mental illness in comparison with locations outside of it. In fact, one of the most controversial films ever produced in the Bay State, Frederick Wiseman's *Titicut Follies*, was banned upon its release in Massachusetts because of the way it portrayed the mentally ill residents of Bridgewater State Hospital—even though the commonwealth declared it was due to privacy issues. Watching the way the staff handles the patients in that film is allegorical to how we're treated by the Bridgewater Triangle—the inmates are already a little bit crazy, but the asylum is only making it worse.

The triangle area was considered to have a certain power long before the English settlers first trekked through it. At its center is the Hockomock Swamp, which at six thousand-plus acres is the second-largest wetland in Massachusetts. At least thirteen rare and endangered species live in the swamplands—and possibly some hereto undiscovered ones as well—and archaeologists have found materials around the swamp that date back some nine thousand years.

The name *Hockomock* comes from the Wampanoag languages, and means "place where spirits dwell." The Wampanoags felt that both good and evil spirits resided near the swamp, which if properly revered could bring great fortune in hunting and fishing but if mistreated could bring doom and destruction.

As civilization has encroached upon it, attempted to develop it and continually misunderstood it, the swamp may have gone into permanent negative mode.

Those who visit the swamp have reported seeing thunderbirds (mysterious birds the size of a full-grown man), pterodactyls, dogs with glowing red eyes, huge snakes, black panthers and, perhaps most notably, a Bigfoot-like creature traipsing about the area.

UFOs have been reported flying over the swamp as far back as May of 1760 and again in 1908. They are commonly sighted throughout the Bridgewater Triangle in modern times, but reports of a "sphere of fire" (according to Pittman's website) appearing over the skies 150 years before the first airplane certainly makes the triangle sightings historic.

With all the mysterious phenomena that take place within the triangle, ghosts actually tend to fall by the wayside when investigating the area.

However, it was within the Bridgewater Triangle that I had my first ghostly experiences.

In my teenage years, I had relatives living in the small town of Halifax, on the outer eastern edge of the Bridgewater Triangle. My aunt and uncle purchased a home that, while not terribly old, stood on what had been farmland since the first settlers came in the late 1600s. It was country living at its finest, and I often spent time there during the summer.

During their first years there, it became apparent that they weren't alone in that house. Shadows would move along the walls down the hallway. Faucets would turn themselves on in the middle of the night. The door to the closet in a child's bedroom would fly open no matter how many times he'd made sure it was shut tight.

I experienced it for myself firsthand the night the bulkhead doors to the basement continually slammed open and shut, even though we had secured them with a wooden two-by-four between the interior handles. Each time we ran down there and locked it down, I still thought we were just the victims of some prank—until I walked down and could still see the heavy metal doors flopping open and shut on their own in the still night air. The topic of the paranormal was something in which I'd always been interested, but after that night, it consumed me. I would soon find out that the ghosts of the SouthCoast were all around me. I just had to know where to look.

CHAPTER 3
THE WHERE

With all the stuffy science and background information out of the way, now we can get to the fun part: the ghosts themselves.

With the current paranormal media explosion—everything from books, magazines, reality television shows and films like *Paranormal Activity*—it's becoming more accepted to talk about things like ghosts and hauntings. While many still scoff at such a notion, and others may deem it a slight against their chosen belief system, it's still easier today to walk into your public library and ask the reference librarian about ghost stories from your town than it was ten or twenty years ago.

With that in mind, more and more historical locations are willing to use ghosts as a way to connect with a new, younger audience. You need only do a Google search for "historic ghost tours" to see there's practically one in every city and quite a few towns as well. On my radio show, *Spooky Southcoast*, we've come up with a simple saying that summarizes how we view the place of the paranormal in learning about our past: come for the ghosts, stay for the history.

That's the approach we'll take with *Ghosts of the SouthCoast* as well. While others might try to spook readers with chilling tales of terrorizing screams and ghostly hands knocking on the window, in this volume we'll treat the ghosts for exactly what they are: a direct link to our past, a (formerly) living example of the SouthCoast's diverse history. Throughout, I'll try to offer some personal insights and anecdotes from my own adventures investigating the paranormal in the area, and you'll see they're more likely to raise an eyebrow than they are the hair on the back of your neck.

Still, it might not be a bad idea to lock the front door and turn on all the lights as we head into the unknown.

WAREHAM AND BUZZARDS BAY

The town of Wareham lies along the beginnings of the Cape Cod Canal, and its official nickname is Gateway to Cape Cod. It's considered the easternmost edge of what we call the SouthCoast and has as much in common with its Cape-side counterparts as it does with the other SouthCoast communities.

Wareham was originally named Agawam after the Wampanoag tribe that inhabited it. In 1666, the Plymouth colony purchased Agawam from the Indians and later renamed it Wareham in homage to a town in Dorset, England, of the same name. It was incorporated as its own town in 1739.

Within Wareham's borders is the coastal village of Onset. Its seaside bluffs and abundant ocean view made it a destination point for the wealthy and the famous in the early 1900s, and at one time it was known as Hollywood East for the celebrities that would often vacation there.

In its own way, Wareham still has a connection with the Hollywood of today. Oscar-winning actress Geena Davis, who starred in such paranormally themed films as *Beetlejuice* and *The Fly*, is a Wareham native.

The Fearing Tavern

One of the oldest structures in Wareham is the Fearing Tavern. Along with having perhaps the coolest name of any haunted location, it's also a spot where the ghosts are directly related to its history.

The original part of the building dates back to 1690, when it was built by Isaac Bump and his family. Israel Fearing later took ownership and added another portion to the building in 1765, and it remained in his family for hundreds of years. During its long history, the sixteen-room Fearing Tavern has served as a tavern, courthouse, town hall, post office, private residence and is now a museum housing a collection of antiques from the seventeenth, eighteenth and early nineteenth centuries.

Wareham's Fearing Tavern has a mysterious past as well as a haunting present.

As a Wareham resident and host of a paranormal radio show, I was able to convince the town's historical society to allow myself and some colleagues the opportunity to conduct a paranormal investigation of the tavern, the first time it had ever been done. We had heard stories about a ghostly woman seen sitting in a rocking chair by schoolchildren on a tour, but we mainly wanted the chance to investigate it because of its long and rich history.

I had an opportunity to talk with one of the last residents to live in the tavern before it was turned over to the town in the 1950s. He told me that when he lived there with his family as a child, it was just like any other house in town. He had indoor plumbing, electricity and all the other modern amenities of the time. However, in 1958, the historical society restored it to its original colonial condition, and it remains so today.

There are two unique features to the tavern that are a prominent if unsolved part of its history. The first is a hidden room wedged between two bedrooms on the second floor, and the other is that two black bands are painted around its dual white chimneys and have been since colonial times. Many historians believe that the black bands were a sign that the owners were loyal to the British crown during the Revolution, and the hidden room was used to hide Redcoats from the militia. The other school of thought is that the black bands indicated that the home was part of the Underground Railroad in the 1800s, and that the hidden room was used to house escaped slaves en route to Canada.

In my research, I found at least one other home less than a mile from the tavern that had a similar hidden room, this one in the basement. The owners of that particular home had passed down a story of its use as part of the Underground Railroad, as the home had not been built in the time of the Revolution.

Adding to the legend is the rumor of a hidden tunnel under the foundation of the tavern that leads under the street and comes out under the Tremont Nail factory across the way. During the early part of Wareham's history, a cotton mill stood on the site of the current nail factory, right along the shore. Historians speculate that aside from Loyalist or Underground Railroad implications, such a tunnel might have also been used to carry goods back and forth from the tavern to the water.

It is this rumored tunnel that led to one of the more frightening pieces of evidence of the paranormal I've ever experienced. In our investigation of the tavern, we brought along our good friend and EVP specialist Mike Markowicz. EVP is an acronym that stands for electronic voice phenomena, when ghosts can imprint their own voices on audio recordings through manipulation of energy. These voices are not audible during the course of the investigation but are discovered later upon review of the tapes.

Mike has his own unique system of conducting EVP research, and it includes using ten condenser microphones (like you would find in our radio studio) strategically located throughout the location, tied into one central mixing board and then recorded digitally on a laptop. With his ultrasensitive and high-end equipment, it's not uncommon for Mike to leave a location with dozens of solid EVPs, while other investigators using hand-held recorders might be lucky to come across one or two prime examples in their entire career. It was with this equipment that Mike captured a statement that to this day sends a shiver down my spine.

In the basement of the tavern, our team was searching for evidence of this supposed underground tunnel. Matt Moniz, my *Spooky Southcoast* cohost and a paranormal investigator for more than twenty years, began using a broomstick to thump on the concrete portion of the floor to check for hollow spots. When we found one, we immediately began clearing off the dirt from the floor with our feet, making one large collective swooshing sound. Within that sound, perhaps using the kinetic energy of our motion to draw power, an evil sounding voice came through to make a startling pronouncement: "Hey Ashford…I killed Grandpa, Ash. I just knew that you'd feel the pain!"

Our sweeping motion stopped for a moment, before we picked it back up again. Once again, the voice came through with creepiness: "Then consider [*sic*] it…a gift."

This didn't sound like a confession; it sounded like the gleeful remembrance of a twisted individual. Although no historical society records mention any Ashford associated with the Fearing Tavern property, whatever happened may have been something deemed too heinous to keep in the permanent record in those days.

Other strange phenomena have been captured during our investigations into the tavern: a glowing orb of light dubbed Tinkerbelle caught on video darting among nineteenth-century toys in an empty room; a loud and animated conversation clearly heard between two women on the second floor of the tavern while everyone who was in the building was listening to it intently from the first floor kitchen; an EVP of a young girl's voice inquiring in sing-song innocence "Wanna play dress-up?"; another of an iron gate being slammed shut when no such gate is believed to have ever been a part of the tavern.

This is just a small sampling of the evidence we've captured in this location that has led us to dub it Wareham's most historic haunt. Some of the EVPs captured also make reference to the Revolutionary War and the king of England.

The Revolutionary War wasn't the last time the British visited the tavern, either. In 1814, the British warship *Nimrod* invaded Wareham. The most feared vessel during the war between the young United States and the mighty Great Britain, the *Nimrod* came to town to investigate allegations that the cotton mill was producing weaponry and that privateers were looming in the waters around town. The British troops landed in Wareham, set fire to the mill, stopped in for a drink at the tavern and marched back to their ship. However, Captain Israel Fearing wasn't about to let them get away easily and cornered them with about a dozen men at his side. The British troops then took two citizens hostage in order to ensure their safe escape and later dropped the hostages off at

Cromesett Neck on western edge of Wareham before heading back into the waters of Buzzards Bay.

Some say that at night, if you're around the area of the Tremont Nail factory and the Fearing Tavern, you can still hear the British soldiers' calls and the firing of their muskets.

Ghosts of Glen Charlie

In East Wareham, there is the long and winding Glen Charlie Road that connects the town to the southern tip of Plymouth. Once an area heavily populated by Indians, it is surrounded by ponds that feed off the Agawam River as well as a large cranberry bog, a recreational campground and a few wooded spots that have yet to be developed. It makes for a spooky drive late at night through its twists and turns that force you to drive at a slower pace and leave you susceptible to a spirit sighting.

That's exactly the case around the *S* curve of road that rides alongside the cranberry bog, where the ghosts of three cranberry workers are often spotted crossing Glen Charlie Road to the waters across the way. According to legend, they were immigrants who were killed in some sort of harvesting accident on the bog in the early part of the twentieth century, and their spirits seem to be a residual haunt that often frighten motorists.

Wampanoag spirits are also said to haunt the Glen Charlie area, as is the mysterious Woman in White. She is often reported strolling through the yards of homes near Glen Charlie Pond, with her long, flowing gown glowing with a luminescence that appears as bright as the moonlight itself.

Glen Charlie was also in the vicinity of the Agawam Nail Works, begun by Samuel Tisdale in 1836. It was one of many such factories in Wareham that utilized the bog iron found in abundance in the manufacturing of iron tools and goods. Agawam ceased operation in 1869 upon Tisdale's death. On December 3, 1885, the *Boston Daily Globe* printed a story about the Glen Charlie area, mostly about how it was a favorite spot of American statesman Daniel Webster in his day. However, there was this interesting passage about the observances of those who lived near the old nail works even after its closure:

> *Whenever a tempestuous storm is raging in this locality, a most singular*
> *specter exhibits itself about the old place. In the mill, life and activity seemed*

to reign. The old furnaces, as in years past, are seen again in full blast; while from the stacks fire is shooting heavenward. In the works everything appears full of life. Bosses and firemen that have long ago passed away can again be seen busy at their respective duties. The huge old rolls groan and snap under their heavy weight, while the old familiar "side" waterwheel is again observed at these times running like a race-horse.

The article goes on to state that everyone who occupied the home near the site of the works reported the exact same occurrence. While the nail works itself is now long gone, its spectral occupants continue to roam Glen Charlie.

Across town in what was formerly known as South Wareham was the Weweantic Iron Company. Originally built in 1835, it later burned to the ground after a deadly explosion that killed many of the ironworkers. Almost immediately after came reports of their tortured souls wandering the grounds of the works. Each time the company rebuilt—there were three more fires after the first explosion—the works would burn again in devastating fashion. Locals began to speak of some sort of curse over the land where the works was built, that it might have been a sacred Indian site at one time.

The Glowing Woman

Along the shores of Onset Bay, there are reports of a female apparition often seen walking along the beach. She looks toward the water, perhaps awaiting a returning love out at sea. She is often reported with a glowing blue hue about her. What makes this particular report interesting is that the same type of apparition has also been seen across the Cape Cod Canal in the town of Sandwich. Is it possible that this same female spirit crosses the canal, ethereally oblivious to its rapidly moving currents?

The Houses of the Unholy

Near the center of Onset is a collection of athletic fields and a playground known as Lopes Field. Surrounding the complex are a number of dilapidated former summer homes that have not been inhabited for some time. Families at the playground, and often teenagers who visit it on warm summer nights, report shadow figures darting among the houses and the sounds of breaking glass filling the night air, even though few windows actually remain in many of the homes.

Those who have dared to enter the homes are shocked at the sight that awaits them. In the center of one house is a large pentagram drawn on the floor, leading to speculation that the abandoned homes have been used for some sort of satanic worship.

In reality, the old homes are not that far from a neighborhood that used to be known for a high amount of drug trafficking until a recent crackdown by the Wareham Police Department. What's more likely is that heroin users would break into these homes in order to get their fix in privacy, and that would account for much of the shadowy movement and broken glass. The pentagram is also likely the work of some of the teenagers who have gone into the homes in order to fool around and keep the legend going.

The Weirdness of Wickets Island

Overlooking the bluffs of Onset Bay is the statue of a Native American maiden, who has drawn more than her share of odd glances because, well, she's bare-breasted. But what few stop to ponder is exactly what she's looking out toward.

In Onset Bay stands Wickets Island, four-and-a-half acres of land that has had a tragic history. In some of Wareham's earliest histories, the island was owned by an Indian named Jabez Wicket who lived on the island in the late 1700s and was passed on to another Indian named Jesse Webquish. The island was eventually sold for private use, and a grand home was built, standing until it burned down in 1980.

The Wampanoags of today, however, believe that the sale of the island was actually illegal, and that they are still the rightful owners of Wickets. They cite the Indian Non Intercourse Act of 1790, which states that lands owned by Indians couldn't be sold to the state or to non-Indians unless approved by Congress. Since that never happened, they believe the island to still be under their control.

In 1815, a violent storm eroded away much of Wickets Island and, according to Daisy Lovell's *Glimpses of Early Wareham*, published in 1970 by the historical society, many ancient Indian graves were washed into the bay. Perhaps it is the restless spirits of these Wampanoags who are often sighted to this day staring back at the mainland from along Wickets's shores.

There are no structures remaining on Wickets and no inhabitants on the island, but occasional ghostly smoke is seen billowing from phantom fires. Those who have been out in the bay in their boats for night cruises often report the sound of drums beating from behind the trees on the island.

The island was sold in 2003 after the family that last owned it had to sell it as part of bankruptcy proceedings. It was purchased for the bargain price of $625,000 by a developer who has since put it on the market for $2.6 million but is also hoping to construct a home on the island that will fetch up to $5 million when completed.

It'll be interesting to see if whoever spends all that money to purchase Wickets Island can endure the spirits that claimed it as their home first.

Getting in the Spirit

Anyone who visits Onset is taken aback by its beauty. Alongside its glistening shoreline stand amazing Victorian homes, still as splendid today as they were when they were built more than one hundred years ago.

Sporting the Queen Anne style that was popular during the Victorian age, the homes look like gigantic dollhouses in the middle of a picturesque seaside village. Most visitors to Onset just figure they're part of the village's past in which the wealthy and powerful would summer along its bluffs—but there's something more spiritual to it than that.

In the world of the paranormal, March 31, 1848, is a very important date. It's when the two Fox sisters—Maggie, age fifteen, and Kate, age twelve—began experiencing strange rappings on the walls of their home in Hydesville, New York. They eventually became celebrated mediums and helped give birth to the spiritualism movement, in which followers believed the dead could speak through mediums and offer advice from the great beyond. Spiritualism enjoyed a long run from that fateful date until well into the early part of the twentieth century, and it peaked in the late 1800s with more than eight million followers in the United States and Europe.

Many followers of the spiritualist movement were upper-class citizens, people in high positions and of great wealth. It is rumored that Abraham Lincoln attended many séances around Washington, D.C., and that he allowed his wife, Mary Todd Lincoln, to have mediums present in the White House.

In 1877, a group of wealthy businessmen known as the Onset Bay Grove Association saw the resort area that was then known as Pine Point as the perfect place to build a spiritualist camp. The association had taken its name from *Oknowam* (another form of Agawam), which was Wampanoag for "the sandy landing place." The camp was dedicated on June 14 of that year and became one of the country's premier spiritualist camps, rivaling Lily Dale in New York for its sense of community and Victorian splendor.

However, rising skepticism of the spiritualist movement soon put a target squarely on Onset. A book called *Some Account of the Vampires of Onset, Past and Present*, published by the Press of S. Woodbury and Company of Boston in 1892, portrayed spiritualism in a negative light, attempting to debunk many popular mediums as frauds and many of the cornerstones of the movement as hoaxes. Of course, none of the material in the book is at all directly related to the Onset camp, but that didn't stop it from tarnishing the camp's image.

To counteract some of the negative publicity of the book, the Onset Bay Grove Association decided to erect a memoriam to the Native Americans whose spirits they believed helped guide them in their lives. In 1894, work was

The On-i-set Wigwam was built in 1893 and is still in use for spiritualist services today.

completed on the On-i-set Wigwam, which would honor the Wampanoag heritage while offering a place for spiritualists to convene and worship. A healing pole in the center of the octagonal wooden structure helped cure what ailed visitors on a physical, emotional and spiritual level.

More than one hundred years later, the wigwam still stands, with the plaque hanging over the entranceway that reads, "Erected to the Memory of the Redmen, 1893. Liberty Throughout the World and Freedom to All Races." Not far from the wigwam, the First Spiritualist Church of Onset still conducts regular services as part of the more modernized version of the Spiritualist Church.

It's no surprise that ghosts should be associated with an area where many share a belief system that actually welcomes and invites their presence. So many stories have come out of the cottages that surround the wigwam and the Victorian houses that dot the waterfront, but unlike other ghost stories in which the spirit is a tragic figure, these spectral visitors are considered old friends there to lend a ghostly guiding hand.

THE TRI-TOWN REGION: MARION, MATTAPOISETT AND ROCHESTER

Just west of Wareham is what is known to locals as the Tri-Town region, consisting of Marion, Mattapoisett and Rochester. It's a unique dichotomy of three towns that in some respects could not be any more different, yet they share a common bond among them.

Originally, the three towns were actually villages under the general domain of Rochester, when Marion was known as Sippican after the Wampanoag tribe that inhabited the area.

Sippican broke off first, incorporating as Marion in 1852 after Revolutionary War hero Francis Marion. It later became a favorite spot of U.S. presidents Grover Cleveland and Franklin Delano Roosevelt. Mattapoisett—a Wampanoag word meaning "a place for rest"—followed suit in 1857. Over time, Marion and Mattapoisett developed as seaside communities with many wealthy residents, while Rochester maintained more of a rural, agricultural identity.

Even today, each town has fewer than six thousand permanent residents, and the small-town feel of each community means they often consider their ghosts to be almost part of the family.

The Ghost of Lillard Hall

Elizabeth Sprague Taber was Marion's greatest benefactor during its formative years. Upon her death, she left instructions in her will for the founding of a private school on the shores of Sippican Harbor on a piece of land she owned. In 1876, Tabor Academy opened, named per her instructions after Mount Tabor near the Sea of Galilee, where the transfiguration of Jesus Christ is said to have taken place.

Tabor Academy has become of one New England's most prestigious schools since its founding, partly due to the guiding hand of Walter Huston Lillard, who served as headmaster of Tabor from 1916 until 1942. During that time, Tabor enjoyed its largest growth, and the freshman dormitory was named Lillard Hall in his honor.

Throughout the years, a legend has developed in which a male student, either homesick or distraught over bad grades, hanged himself on the top floor of Lillard Hall. While there is no official mention of such a suicide at

Lillard Hall at Marion's prestigious Tabor Academy.

Tabor Academy, true believers cite that it happened in the early days of the institution when such things would not be made public.

Reportedly, students living in Lillard Hall can hear strange voices and other sounds coming from the room where the boy hanged himself. The room is still assigned to incoming freshmen, and legend has it that those who stay in the room often suffer from feelings of dread and despair and are also prone to bad grades. Is there something negative that is somehow attached to the location that led the boy to commit suicide? Is his spirit now trapped in limbo and somehow affecting the current residents of where he met his untimely end?

Ellis–Bolles Cemetery

It's all too easy to consider a cemetery to be haunted, but think about it—if you were a ghost, wouldn't the cemetery be the last place you'd want to hang around? It is one thing if, for reasons unknown, a spirit is somehow imprinted to the place where the physical body died. But to think a spirit would want to willingly stay where the body is laid to rest is pretty macabre, even when we're talking about a ghost.

Yet so many cemeteries and graveyards are reputedly haunted, and paranormal investigators just starting out continue to use them as their training ground. But in one Mattapoisett burial ground, the paranormal might not be so benign.

Ellis–Bolles Cemetery gets its name from the Ellis and the Bolles families that make up a majority of the plots, which date back from the early 1800s until around the 1950s. It stands in the middle of a nearly deserted and mostly dirt road called Wolf Island Road that, at night, increases the creepy factor on the way to the cemetery.

The most prominent legend associated with Ellis–Bolles, like most good ghost stories, has its roots in truth. During King Philip's War, the wooded areas of Rochester and Mattapoisett made a strategic hiding point for both sides. It's alleged that in the vicinity of where the cemetery now stands, there was an ambush and the captured prisoners were subsequently hanged from the trees on Wolf Island Road. No one is exactly sure which side ended up on the business end of the noose, and the ghostly shadow figures often reported to be dangling from the branches in modern times offer no indication as to who won that particular scuffle.

The Ellis–Bolles Cemetery has some spooky gravestones and some even spookier legends.

Another Wolf Island Road legend has grown over the years, this one with nothing more than its continued telling to back it up. According to the tale, in the early 1970s a carload of teenagers were cruising around in a Ford Mustang and went speeding down the dirt road. At some point, the driver rammed his Mustang into a tree and everyone in the car was killed instantly.

According to the legend, if you head out onto Wolf Island Road, park your car and blink your headlights three times, off in the distance you will see another pair of headlights blink back in your direction, before you hear the loud roar of a Mustang's engine and see the headlights speeding toward you, even though you can't quite make out the car to which they belong. You can feel the ghostly vehicle and its occupants as it passes through your car, but by that point the only thing you'll see are taillights fading in the distance out your back window.

Of course, this is also a common story associated with many other graveyards—I know of at least one in Massachusetts that shares a similar lore—but that doesn't stop the locals from passing it on.

In the trips that I've made out to Ellis–Bolles Cemetery, there has never been a phantom Mustang and I have yet to see hanging Wampanoags or colonists in the trees, but I have acquired interesting evidence. When we began *Spooky Southcoast* radio in 2006, cohost Matt Costa and I decided we should check out Ellis–Bolles one night on our way into the WBSM studios. Armed with digital cameras and tape recorders, we spent about an hour poking around not long after the sun had gone down.

In looking at one grave, Matt noticed strange pitting on the granite of the tombstone and pointed it out to me. I responded by saying, "That's weird," and on the audio tape we caught an EVP that sounded to me as if it was a voice repeating the word weird. It had a high-pitched squeak to it, almost as if it was a female voice. It is not uncommon for the voices on EVPs to repeat what the investigator has said, and often times it is done so in a mocking fashion.

We sent the EVP out to different experts to have it analyzed, and what came back was very interesting. One analysis placed it outside the normal human speaking range and determined that was being said was actually something more akin to Marion or Miriam. Now, Ellis–Bolles is only a stone's throw from Marion, so that's one possibility. But we also went back on a return trip along with our show's science advisor, Matt Moniz, and discovered a grave near the spot the EVP was recorded with the name Mary.

On that return trip, the two Matts were investigating a grave with a symbol on it while I was on the other side of the cemetery and we each had a recorder rolling. Matt Costa was recording on analog tape, while Matt Moniz and I each ran digital, albeit at two different settings. When Costa asked Moniz about the symbol, Moniz informed him it was a Freemason symbol. Immediately after, we caught an EVP repeating the word Freemason—on all three recorders. Even more incredibly, I was standing about twenty feet away from the two Matts when it imprinted on my recorder.

Whatever may be present at Ellis–Bolles Cemetery, it definitely seems to have strength greater than that of your usual graveyard ghost.

The Biggest Mystery of Rochester

The town of Rochester is mainly an agricultural community, comprised of cranberry bogs and farms. They have a county fair each year that is a testament to the spirit of community and the blue-collar nature of this farming town.

Another testament is just how tight-lipped they seem to be about many of their ghost stories. Even at a time when talking about the paranormal is almost considered normal, it's hard to get a Rochester resident to open up about any experiences they may have had.

However, I have had a few off-the-record discussions with residents who tell me it's not uncommon to be driving along these rural roads late at night and see spectral beings out walking the fields. While there haven't been strong enough intelligent haunts to put Rochester on the paranormal map, it seems as though there's plenty of residual activity going on.

The other thing that amazes me about Rochester, though, is that these same people who are so reluctant to share their ghost tales are more than willing to describe the mysterious lights they may have seen in the sky one night. With all its open space, Rochester is a prime spot for catching a glimpse of a UFO. So if you're ever in the area, keep your eyes to the skies!

What in Hell's Blazes?

Even though the Hell's Blazes Tavern is technically in Middleboro, it is right along the edge of Rochester, and since Middleboro isn't part of the SouthCoast as we're defining it, we'll allow Rochester to adopt it for a few moments while we discuss another of the area's longest-standing haunts.

Originally built in 1690 (the same year as Wareham's Fearing Tavern), Hell's Blazes was at one point the oldest continuously operating tavern in the United States. However, a 1971 fire and subsequent rebuild may have altered the original tavern—but not its ghosts.

Like the Fearing Tavern, Hell's Blazes has the perfect name for a haunted spot. According to legend, it got its name from the glow cast on the tavern from a nearby smelting furnace back in the colonial era. As stagecoach riders would pull up and see the orange glow cast on the tavern, they'd remark how the place looked "hotter than Hell's blazes." But some believe the name may have something to do with all the restless spirits that roamed the property.

Those who frequented the tavern in its original incarnation have had the most profound experiences, directly connected to nearly three hundred years' worth of history while bellying up to the bar. In the 1960s, the *Standard-Times* newspaper ran a series of articles about an alleged haunting at Hell's Blazes that included slamming doors, rapping and knocking sounds. Workers reported feeling a presence around them, like something

Once the oldest operating tavern in the United States, Hell's Blazes is yet another SouthCoast spot with an appropriately spooky name.

was always standing right behind them but when they would turn around, there was nothing there.

After the fire, only the original carriage house remained. The tavern was rebuilt to look like it was from the 1600s and had much of the rustic charm of the original, but apparently the spirits didn't feel the same way. Reports of ghostly activity waned over the building's last thirty or so years, both among the patrons and the employees. Two former chefs, who each had spent considerable time as the only person in the building during their tenure, both refuted the idea that Hell's Blazes is haunted.

That doesn't sway the belief of another gentleman who told me of his lone paranormal experience coming on the Hell's Blazes property. A serviceman, he was called for an emergency at the tavern late on a spring night in the early 1980s. It was a misty night, and the air was thick and heavy. He knew of the tavern's haunted reputation—his mother had worked there in the 1960s and told tales about stacking dishes neatly at night and coming in to find them in disarray the next morning—but he didn't consider himself a believer until this particular night.

After he was finishing up his repair work, he and his brother got into their truck, started it and prepared to drive down the driveway that led from behind the tavern back to the main road. As they entered the cab of the truck, they saw a woman come from around the end of the building, wearing what he described as a "dark, old-fashioned-looking cloak." He thought she looked as if she was from another time, as she crossed the driveway and entered the double-gated animal pen across the way. But as they drove past, they could see no trace of her—she had vanished in a matter of seconds. That's when he knew he had seen a ghost.

In 2004, Hell's Blazes closed and was sold to the owner of a dismantling company who wanted the site for its land and was rumored to be demolishing the buildings to make room for his salvage yard. The tavern and carriage house still stand, perhaps because the restless spirits within them won't have it any other way.

The Kinsale Inn

Mattapoisett's Kinsale Inn is the quintessential New England seafront inn—and for good reason. It is, according to its website, "the oldest seaside Inn in the nation still operating as an Inn in its original structure."

Built in 1799, the property has also seen a blacksmith shop, general store, a tavern, two separate dwellings and numerous other incarnations in the past two hundred-plus years. Joseph Meigs, the original owner of the property, wanted to build himself a home and provide a spot for weary seafarers to have a drink and enjoy themselves. Two centuries later, that vision is still going strong.

Formerly known as the Mattapoisett Inn, it had established a reputation for excellence even before the Irish Restaurant Company purchased it in 2004 and renamed it the Kinsale Inn. With an emphasis on creating a traditional Irish pub atmosphere, the latest stewards of the historic property are living up to, if not exceeding, the standards set by those before them.

But when they purchased the inn, they got more than just the restaurant, function facilities and guest rooms that were on the deed. They also became stewards of at least two ghosts as well.

The most commonly sighted is that of a sea captain seen in one of the bedroom windows, looking out toward the sea. He also is reported to roam the halls with his heavy boots, making a thunderous sound. According to the inn's website, "the most famous person to live in the Inn was Captain Bryant, a Mattapoisett whaling captain and first Governor of Alaska." According to the site, Bryant would sit on the upper porch of the inn and write his memoirs, which were never found.

This ghost could indeed be that of this Captain Bryant, who is believed to be Charles R. Bryant. Despite numerous Mattapoisett histories listing him as the first governor of Alaska, no official Alaskan histories I could find list him as ever being the head of the territory-turned-state. Instead, Charles R. Bryant served as a special agent of the Treasury in the early days of Alaska, immediately following its purchase from Russia in October of 1867.

The other reported spirit is that of a young girl called Sarah by the locals. For whatever reason, she wanders the hallways of the inn searching for her father. In her never-ending quest, Sarah is known to knock over items, open doors and rattle the bottles at the bar. One medium I spoke with told me of how she went to the Kinsale Inn to dine with her husband, only to have Sarah sit next to her the entire time and look at her forlornly.

FAIRHAVEN AND ACUSHNET

In 1652, the English settlers continued to expand westward from Plymouth and Rochester when they purchased the lands that would eventually become known as Fairhaven and Acushnet. Although it would be another seven years before the two towns would actually be settled, Fairhaven eventually became the home port to many sea captains and their crewmen while Acushnet was more agricultural.

Both Fairhaven and Acushnet were originally part of the Dartmouth settlement, before breaking off and falling under the settlement of New Bedford when the eastern portion of Dartmouth seceded in 1787. Fairhaven and Acushnet later seceded from New Bedford in 1812.

Fort Phoenix

In the late 1700s, Fairhaven was thrust into prominence as the colony prepared for revolution. Just off its shores was the site of the first naval action of the Revolutionary War, when on May 13, 1775, Nathaniel Pope and Daniel Egery, sailing on the sloop *Success* with a crew of twenty-five men, captured two British ships.

Fairhaven's Fort Phoenix has not only the spirits of soldiers past but also some more current ghosts out for a jog along its beaches.

Realizing that Fairhaven's harbor would need protection, construction of Fort Phoenix on Nolscott Point began in June of 1775 under the guidance of Captain Benjamin Dillingham and Eleazer Hathaway, his brother-in-law.

An interesting note about Dillingham—he was a descendent of Edward Dillingham, one of the founders of the Cape Cod town of Sandwich. The original Dillingham House near the center of that town is rumored to be haunted by the spirits of Edward and Branch Dillingham, a later descendent of Edward who hanged himself on the property in 1813. It was formerly a bed and breakfast until it closed to the public in recent years.

A descendent of Benjamin Dillingham bearing the same name later became a prominent businessman on the islands of Hawaii in the late 1800s. There are still stories on the islands about the Dillinghams who haunt them—including Gaylord Dillingham, who was shot down in World War II and whose spirit is legendary among the students at an all-girls' school on the island of Oahu.

Returning to the subject of Fort Phoenix, it was completed in 1777, and on September 5, 1778, the British landed four thousand troops not far from the fort and laid siege to the entire area. Fort Phoenix was abandoned and destroyed by the Redcoats, who also burned down many homes in the village of Fairhaven. Major Israel Fearing marched his company of more than one hundred men from Wareham in order to assist Fairhaven in driving out the British and is recognized for his efforts with a plaque at Fort Phoenix. Of course, he did so by leading his men not from the front of the company but from the rear, threatening to shoot any man who attempted to flee the battle.

Fearing was also the owner of the Fearing Tavern in Wareham and helped defend its shores from the British in the War of 1812, a key figure in SouthCoast paranormal lore.

Fearing's spirit is one of the many associated with Fort Phoenix. The most prominent activity reported is the sound of cannon fire, possibly coming from one of the eleven cannons that were placed strategically around the fort.

There are eleven cannons around Fort Phoenix, including one that John Paul Jones captured from a British ship in the Bahamas.

Although the fort saw action in the Revolutionary War and the War of 1812—it was also commissioned for the Civil War, but never engaged in battle—not all the ghosts reported there are of a military nature. Since the fort area was bequeathed to the town in 1926, it has been a recreational area. One spirit who has been sighted numerous times is that of a jogger who will approach people at the fort and ask the time. The person looks down at their watch or takes out their cellphone in order to check, and when they look up, the jogger has vanished.

The Haunted Library

The Millicent Library was funded by the great benefactor for much of Fairhaven's beautiful structures, Henry Huttleston Rogers. Rogers was a self-made millionaire in the latter half of the nineteenth century and counted among his friends the likes of Mark Twain, Booker T. Washington and Helen Keller, whose college education he financed personally.

Fairhaven's Millicent Library may be haunted by its namesake, among others.

There is another connection between Henry Huttleston Rogers and the paranormal that is perhaps more than just coincidence. Rogers made his fortune in the oil business, most notably as part of John D. Rockefeller's Standard Oil Trust. However, Rogers first got involved in the business at the age of twenty-one and with an investment of six hundred dollars, partnering with a friend to form his own company called the Wamsutta Oil Refinery. While the name is likely a tip of the hat to his SouthCoast roots, perhaps by invoking the name of Massasoit's eldest son, he was awakening the Indian spirits back in his beloved Fairhaven.

In another nod to the odd, Rogers's ruthlessness on Wall Street in his later years led his critics to scoff that the initials in H.H. Rogers actually stood for Hell Hound.

In Fairhaven, however, the man was beloved for the generosity he showed the town.

The library was constructed in the 1890s as a tribute to Millicent Gifford Rogers, who passed away in 1890 at the tender age of seventeen. Because of her love of books and learning, Rogers decided to erect a great library in her honor, which opened to the public on January 30, 1893.

As part of a memoriam for Millicent, the library features a stained-glass window bearing her likeness in angelic form under an image of William Shakespeare and encircled by the names of prominent American poets. The window art depicts Millicent as muse for these great writers, but she's also the muse for the many ghost stories that surround the library that bears her name.

Some of the stories that have circulated over the years include the ghostly specter of Millicent Rogers walking through the library, glowing with a brilliant blue hue. People also have claimed to hear her laughter reverberating through the building.

Many of the stories originate with the myth that Rogers buried his daughter in the foundation of the library. Fueling that myth is that the dedication ceremony for the library's cornerstone took place at 6:00 a.m. on a Monday with only the family and a clergyman present. When the library officially opened and the stained-glass window was unveiled, again it was only the family present. The public services took place in the Congregational Church.

In conducting an investigation and writing a subsequent article for the *Standard-Times* in October of 2006, library director Carolyn Longworth and

The stained-glass window at the library features William Shakespeare and Millicent Rogers in angelic forms.

archivist Debbie Charpentier denied the claim of Millicent being buried in the foundation, and Peter Reid, superintendent of Riverside Cemetery, confirmed her remains are in the Rogers family mausoleum at that site.

Even if Millicent Rogers isn't beneath the beautiful building, other spirits may be present. Some have claimed to have seen a woman dressed all in black running her fingers across the books on the shelves, and others suggest that a man with a tweed jacket, purple bow tie and small, round glasses is often seen mopping the basement floors. The legend is that he's the ghost of a janitor who died after slipping on a wet floor and that his footsteps can also be heard on the spiral staircase that extends from the basement to the library's tower. Many have claimed to encounter his spirit, including psychics and a Native American gentleman visiting from Seattle.

It is this spirit that many believe is responsible for much of the activity experienced at the library, including fire alarms going off for no apparent reason in the middle of the night and other electrical anomalies. In the course of my own investigation, alongside *Spooky Southcoast* cohost and producer Matt Costa, we experienced an unexplainable incident in which a light flickered on and off a few times in the basement, directly over Matt's head with no one else present on the floor and with the light switch within his sight. Not exactly proof of the paranormal, but when we did flick the switch, we saw that it was actually connected to two lights, and only the one directly over him had been affected. The basement and pretty much the entire building are comprised of granite, which could be storing and feeding the paranormal activity.

Another legend associated with the Millicent Library is that the spirit of Hetty Green haunts the Millicent Library because one of her hats rests among the library's artifacts. Green was the first woman to rule the American financial world, earning the nickname of the Witch of Wall Street. She was

Visitors to the Rogers Room often report that the portraits change expressions.

also notoriously frugal, and even though her wealth in modern dollars would make her the wealthiest woman in U.S. history, she is in the Guinness Book of World Records as the World's Greatest Miser. While the hat did at one time rest in the library's archives, it hasn't been there in quite some time.

The Rogers Room houses various artifacts and documents related to the history of the Rogers family, dominated by the huge portraits of H.H. Rogers, his mother and grandmother. Hanging on the far wall of the room, it's said that if you talk directly to the portraits, their expressions change as a result of the conversation. Indeed, the portraits are extremely lifelike, with eyes that seem to follow as one moves across the room. From different angles, the stoic frowns of the women can appear to have the creeping corners of a grin. Cold spots are often reported in this room as well, but it is actually the only room in the library with air conditioning, in order to preserve the artifacts inside.

Despite all these potential ghosts inside, many feel the Millicent Library is haunted without ever having to step foot inside. Built in the Italian-renaissance style by renowned architect Charles Brigham, the library's

This grotesque was removed during renovations and now sits in the library director's office.

exterior is decorated with the gargoyles and grotesques that were popular at the time, placed on buildings to ward off evil spirits. There are also griffins, carvings and other such embellishments throughout the inside as well.

One of those original exterior grotesques—said to be the Greek mythological figure Pan but bearing a striking resemblance to Satan—had to be taken down and replaced with a replica. The original now resides in Longworth's office, and the library used it as a mascot on a T-shirt they had printed. Soon after, according to Longworth herself, employees of the library began having bad things happen in their lives—accidents, financial misfortunes and even the death of the janitor occurred within months of the grotesque moving to its new home. Employees then permanently placed a small Bible atop its head and, at the suggestion of a psychic, burned frankincense in the four corners of the building.

The Castle on the Hill

Many of Fairhaven's finest structures were gifts of H.H. Rogers. Aside from the Millicent Library, he also gave the town a grammar school, the Unitarian Church, the town hall and other improvements. But the one landmark that looms largest is Fairhaven High School, often referred to as the Castle on the Hill.

Built in 1906, it still remains one of the most beautiful and ornate public schools ever built. An addition in the early part of the twenty-first century was constructed for space and to get the building up to code, yet great effort was made to ensure the new part of the building remained true to the atmosphere and design of the original. The result is a seamless blend of a cutting-edge education within historic halls.

It is in those halls that many of the ghost stories associated with Fairhaven High take place.

The most frequent reports involve phantom cold spots that pop up inexplicably around the school, even on the warmest of days. Sometimes, these cold spots act as a precursor to more overt activity, as if the spirit is summoning strength to be able to move an object or make a loud banging sound. One student told me that among the student body, the feeling of a cold spot is usually considered an "uh-oh" moment for fear of what is to follow.

Another student, who as a member of a certain after-school club has had significant opportunities to be in the building after hours when very few

Fairhaven High School, Henry Huttleston Rogers's Castle on the Hill.

students or staff is present, told me of a book that mysteriously dropped from the third floor down a long winding staircase to just in front of where she was standing on the first floor. If she had been standing just a few feet in the wrong direction, what is mostly viewed as benign poltergeist activity could have proved fatal.

Poltergeist, by the way, is a German phrase meaning "noisy ghost." The concept has been around for hundreds of years, and in some incarnations, it's believed that the poltergeist is a spirit unto itself and has no connection to the soul of a human being. In the last fifty or so years, however, research has instead suggested that poltergeist activity could actually be subliminal manifestations of a prepubescent child. More typically associated with females, the activity is actually unintentional psychokinetic activity—manipulating objects with the mind—that comes as a result of hormonal changes and eventually wears off with time.

The gothic detail of Fairhaven High School, home of the Blue Devils.

Cross-Cultural Ghosts

One of the items that draws claims of paranormal activity in the Millicent Library is the samurai sword in the Rogers Room, but it's more likely the stories have grown over the fact that it seems very out of place for Fairhaven—unless you understand the history of how it got there. Even if the ghost story is mostly hogwash, the tale is interesting enough to tell here.

In 1841, a fourteen-year-old peasant boy named Manjiro Nakahama and four friends were shipwrecked off the southern coast of Japan while on a fishing trip. They were rescued by Captain William H. Whitfield of Fairhaven and his crew. They brought them to safety on the Hawaiian island of Oahu (where Benjamin Dillingham's descendents would soon settle) while Whitfield brought Manjiro back to Fairhaven, where he became known as John Manjiro, the first Japanese person to live in America. With the Whitfield family, Manjiro received an education and became a top-notch sailor, eventually setting out to sea once again.

Manjiro eventually arrived in San Francisco just at the dawn of the gold rush and became a wealthy man. He went back and found his friends who were left in Hawaii and they all returned to Japan. Although the policy of the isolationist Japanese people was to execute anyone who left the country, Manjiro and his friends were spared and he provided the Japanese government with tales of the wondrous life in America. He played a key role in Japan, eventually opening up to relations with the West, and he often returned to the United States as a *hatamoto*—a representative samurai—in his later years.

On July 4, 1918, his son, Dr. Toichiro Nakahama, and Japanese ambassador Kikujiro Ishii presented the town of Fairhaven with the samurai sword that now rests in the Millicent Library, part of an ongoing friendship between the town and the Land of the Rising Sun. It is a relationship that still remains in modern times as well. In October of 1987, Japanese crown prince Akihito and his wife, Princess Michiko, visited Fairhaven, and the town has a sister city in Tosashimizu, Japan.

When Japanese tourists visit the SouthCoast, one of their destination points is the grave of Captain Whitfield in Riverside Cemetery, often to leave gifts and give thanks to him for his kindness to Manjiro. Do the Japanese, though, know something about his grave that we do not? The Japanese, after all, are a culture in which ghosts play a very large role. They openly believe in the spirits of the deceased and revere and honor them with special ceremonies. Perhaps they are there to communicate with the captain, just as their fellow countryman did more than 150 years ago.

Don't Touch that Dial

The following story has become more than just a great ghost story; it's also spread to the status of urban legend. Whether it originated on the SouthCoast is unknown, but similar tales have popped up elsewhere.

Nichols House is a nursing home in Fairhaven on Main Street, near the Riverside Cemetery where Millicent Rogers lies and just down the road from Fairhaven High School. As the story goes, an elderly woman was a resident of Nichols House and her favorite time of the day was the late afternoon, when she could sit in the front parlor of the house and listen to her beloved classical music station. Yet a certain orderly who had no love for this woman would often come in and change the station to blaring rock music, perhaps to intentionally annoy her. One day, she reached her boiling point and had enough of his constant rock and roll torture, and she ran out the front door of the nursing home and into the street, where she was immediately struck and killed by a passing car.

The legend goes that as you drive past the nursing home, if you tune your car's radio station to 102.9 FM—the signal of the rock station the orderly changed the radio to each time—the signal will fade out and be replaced by classical music, as the old woman gets her way from the great beyond.

From the moment I first heard this story, I knew what had sparked it; 102.9 FM, the dial setting for rock station WPXC is one step up on the FM dial from 102.5, which for about fifty-five years was home to classic rock station WCRB until that station moved down the dial in 2009. WPXC originates on Cape Cod, while WCRB broadcast out of Boston, and Fairhaven seemed like the perfect spot for the signals to become crossed somehow to allow one station to bleed into the other.

When I went out to try it, that's exactly what happened, and still does to this day—although 102.5 is now country station WKLB, and Nichols House has been renamed the Royal at Fairhaven. The names and station formats may have changed, but the legend lives on.

That Dam Woman

Acushnet comes from the Wampanoag *acushnea*, which has been translated by some to mean "at the head of the river" or "resting place along the river." One interesting translation, which comes from Maurice DesJardins, suggests that Acushnet in the Wampanoag means "a place where we get to the other side."

Now, if that doesn't sound like a paranormal hot spot, I don't know what does. If Acushnet is a place to get to the Other Side, it's also a place that the Other Side likes to get to. Take, for example, the spectral woman who is often seen taking in the view around the Hamlin Road Dam. She is said to be seen in the early morning hours, just as the sun rises, and described as a peaceful and benign spirit.

The same can't be said for another ghostly woman seen farther up the Acushnet River. This spirit often frightens away those who see her, with her animalistic behavior along the shores of the river and a name that is crudely carved into her back, yet no one has been able to get close enough to read what it says.

The Samuel West House

At a time when many men of God in Massachusetts were all about hellfire and brimstone, the Reverend Dr. Samuel West was of a different breed. Viewed as a liberal who was more akin to the later Unitarian movement, West would have made an imposing figure on the pulpit had he stuck to the Puritan preaching style. He was a large man—over six feet tall and weighed more than two hundred pounds, but often appeared disheveled and dirty. He was a man of little means, making a meager salary with the First Congregational Society in Dartmouth (in present-day New Bedford) after being ordained in 1761.

The property that would come to bear his name passed hands quite a bit beginning in 1742, with the oldest part of the current building being built sometime prior to 1775. West came to own it in 1785, as he recovered judgment from a Thomas Crandon and took control of the property as part of that judgment—but whether he actually resided there is unknown. West

The staircase at the Samuel West House leads to the haunted third floor. *Courtesy of Christopher Balzano.*

had actually taken his congregation to court over his pay, and his ownership of the Acushnet property may have been related to that. It is believed that at one time, there was a church and a graveyard on the property, so he may have actually just been granted the property on which he was already serving in the church.

In the 1920s, the house was used as a funeral home but fell into disrepair when it became a private residence again years later.

Katie and Johnny now live in the home with their three children. The upstairs is occupied by another couple, while the third floor—the attic space—is reserved for the ghosts. But that doesn't stop them from coming down and interacting with the living residents.

Since Katie moved in, she's tried to make improvements about the house, and each time it seems as though more spirits awake. It's not uncommon in the paranormal to see activity spike as repairs are being done to a location; ghosts become accustomed to their surroundings or have an attachment to the way it was when they were alive, and changes to it often invoke their ire.

Even when they're not renovating, however, the family has endured amazing levels of paranormal activity. From phantom footsteps to full-fledged apparitions, the phenomena in the Samuel West House run the complete gamut. Voices are often heard in unoccupied rooms, bells will ring on their own and balls of light have materialized out of thin air and then dissipated just as quickly. Unattached voices will call out residents of the house by name. Horrible smells, like something out a sewer or a garbage can, will permeate the house with no known source. And, above all, *nobody* wants to go in the attic because of how strong the activity is up there.

Katie contacted author and analytical folklorist Christopher Balzano when he put out word through his website, the Massachusetts Paranormal Crossroads (www.masscrossroads.com), that he was looking for stories of paranormal activity in the area. Balzano and a group of paranormal investigators, including *Spooky Southcoast* cohost and science advisor Matt Moniz, have since spent the past several years documenting what haunts the West house.

What they've found is some of the most intriguing evidence of the existence of ghosts. As documented in Balzano's book *Picture Yourself Ghost Hunting* and the accompanying DVD, EVPs are captured with relative ease in the house. The spirits actually speak to the investigators by name, both aloud and through EVPs, and ask about them when they haven't been there in a while. Talcum powder sprinkled on the floor or bookshelf is soon littered with handprints, footprints and written messages even when nobody is in the room to make them.

Even Balzano's DVD was affected by the ghosts of the Samuel West House, with EVPs appearing in the footage captured during the editing process. In one particular scene, Balzano's camera is being drained of all its battery power as a disembodied voice imprints itself on the camera's audio, which sounds like an upset male saying something about a death in a plane crash. Andrew Lake of Greenville Paranormal Research in Rhode Island, who was present on the investigation and edited the film, confirmed through newspaper research that a plane crash occurred very close to the home in 1957.

Over time, Katie and Johnny have learned to live with the ghosts, and the ghosts have learned to live with them. While it can still become unnerving on occasion, the spirits of the Samuel West House have become a part of their family.

NEW BEDFORD

New Bedford is known as the Whaling City because of its deep heritage in the whaling industry. Made famous by Herman Melville's 1851 classic *Moby Dick*, it still remains today as the number one fishing port in the world.

Originally part of the Dartmouth settlement, New Bedford seceded and incorporated under its new name in 1787. As the whaling industry helped it grow, it officially became a city in 1847. Around that time, New Bedford experienced an immigration boom, mostly from Portugal. The influence of Portuguese culture is still strong within the city today.

New Bedford was also a significant location in African American history. The famous abolitionist Frederick Douglass, a former slave, settled in New Bedford in 1838. It was here that the seeds were planted for the crusader against racial injustice that Douglass would eventually become.

The Haunted Armory

In paranormal circles, New Bedford is probably best known for the National Guard Armory on Sycamore Street, because it was featured in an early but memorable episode of the SyFy Channel show *Ghost Hunters*, which

The haunted armory in New Bedford, as seen on the SyFy Channel's *Ghost Hunters*.

starred, among others, New Bedford native Steve Gonsalves. In the episode, Pilgrim Films sound man Frank deAngelis is knocked to the ground when an unseen spirit passes through him. According to members of the Atlantic Paranormal Society (TAPS, the featured team on *Ghost Hunters*) that I've spoken with, deAngelis was not a believer in the paranormal prior to that experience. It disturbed him so badly that he left the crew of the program shortly thereafter.

The castlelike armory was built in 1903 but was used less and less through the 1990s as it fell into disrepair. It was eventually shut down and put on the auction block, but nobody has yet come up with the funds necessary to take ownership of the property and then make the necessary repairs to get it up to code.

The current condition of the building is even more of a nightmare than the ghosts that haunt it, as an upper floor has reportedly rotted away completely, crashing into the level below it. Flooding is another problem as well.

When it was still staffed by the National Guard, the guardsmen would often report seeing a black-hooded figure lurking about in the shadows, and an unseen force that would shove them from behind. Whatever it was also had enough strength to violently slam some of the heavy steel doors within the armory.

The building is now closed permanently, and trespassers will be prosecuted to the fullest extent of the law.

The Ghouls of the Schools

Numerous students of New Bedford schools who have heard our radio show have contacted us to say they've had experiences in their school. One elementary school is rumored to be haunted by a former principal that died on the school grounds, although there is no verification of any such death.

Other rumored but unconfirmed deaths are said to be the cause of alleged haunts at New Bedford High School. The activity reported includes slamming lockers and sinks that turn themselves on. There is also a story about someone who hanged himself in the projection booth of the high school auditorium, whose ghost remains behind, keeping an eternal watch over the stage. Lights going on and off and curtains closing on its own are some of the most frequent reports associated with this spirit.

Nothing to See at the Z

Ironically, the same story is attached to the historic Zeiterion Theater in downtown New Bedford. The claim is that shortly after the 1923 opening of the venue, profits weren't as great as anticipated and, distraught, the owner of the theater hanged himself in the projection booth. According to an internet report, there are rooms without doors, doors without rooms and hallways that lead to nowhere.

Considering how cozy the theater already is, it's doubtful anyone would construct a venue in such a fashion. In 2007, when I inquired about it, management at the Z denied any such claims—although they wouldn't let me snoop around to check it out for myself, either.

Wamsutta Club

Not far from the Zeiterion Theater is the Wamsutta Club, one of the finest private clubs in the country. It originally was organized by Charles Warren Clifford in 1866 as a baseball club, but it wasn't long before it grew into a

The Wamsutta Club in New Bedford has its own high-class hauntings.

social club and was formally chartered in 1889. Over the years it was housed in a few different locations before settling in the former mansion of James Arnold, its current location, in 1919. The mansion was built in 1921 and has since been expanded to accommodate the club's members.

Not only was the club moving into classy digs, but they were classy digs that had been owned by classy people. Arnold had been involved in the whaling industry and had amassed a great fortune, which he used to fund his lavish gardens that he would open to the public. His wife, Sara, the daughter of his business partner William Rotch, was also known for her work with the poorer citizens of New Bedford.

In its time, the Wamsutta Club has featured some of the most prominent citizens of New Bedford in its membership—from the whaling magnates to those who made their fortunes in the booming textile business of the early 1900s, the club was a who's who of the Whaling City.

However, the Great Depression meant the club had to lower its membership dues and, in doing so, opened its doors to a much wider portion of SouthCoast citizens. Even today, the club is affordable enough for middle-class families to enjoy a taste of the upper-class life.

For as long as its history may be, there are actually few reports of paranormal activity that come out of the club. That may be more because of the tight-lipped nature of private club membership, but Eric LaVoie, the founder of Dartmouth Anomalies Research Team (DART), heard from an employee of the club that the place was actually quite haunted. He reported hearing the service elevator going off on its own, when he and the person he was working with were the only people in the building. He also reported that many employees refused to go in the basement or the boiler room because they always feel as if they are being watched.

After contacting club manager Cindy Bouchard, Eric received clearance from the board of directors to become the first paranormal team to investigate the Wamsutta Club.

Eric assembled a team that included Linda Lynch of Veils Edge Paranormal, Andrew Lake of Greenville Paranormal Research and EVP researcher Mike Markowicz, and the investigation was filmed for a DVD by Aldimar Video Productions and covered by a local journalist named Bob Eckstrom. With access to areas that are even off-limits to the paying members, the investigators said they felt no uneasy feelings anywhere in the building—except in the basement and the boiler room. They detected no high electromagnetic fields, or EMF, that would cause people to have the sensation of being watched. Also while investigating down there, they captured a number of intriguing EVPs, including one that said "don't be afraid," another that said "it's evil; pick up the hatchet" and one that called Eric by name.

Eric also asked if the spirits minded the investigators being there, to which he received a reply of "I don't" as an EVP.

Another area that proved to be active was the private apartments that are within the club, for those who choose to stay there. One resident described frequently waking up to odd sounds and the feeling of an unseen presence.

Linda, who is a medium, detected the spirit of Sara Arnold still attached to the property as well as the spirit of a man standing near the bar in the Rounder's Club located in the basement. She also reported feeling as though someone had been killed in that downstairs portion and the body was dumped in some sort of river, although she's found nothing in historical records to verify it yet.

Those who had the chance to investigate the Wamsutta Club agree that there is great potential for a residual haunting on the property, and that there may even be a number of intelligent spirits still hanging around. If so, let's hope they've paid their membership dues.

Fort Taber–Fort Rodman

After the British successfully raided and burned much of the SouthCoast's homes in 1778, local merchants started pulling together the funds and manpower necessary to erect some means of protection along the shores of New Bedford Harbor at Clark's Point.

At first, they put up a wooden beacon in 1797; a lighthouse followed in 1804. But, following the War of 1812, the need for better defense had more citizens concerned about protecting the city and its growing whaling industry

Ghostly wars are still raging at the Fort Taber–Fort Rodman complex on the southern tip of New Bedford.

from outside invaders. In the late 1840s, it was decided that a permanent military fort was needed at Clark's Point, but it wasn't until 1857 that they purchased the lands necessary to do so. Meanwhile, the Civil War broke out, and on May 11, 1861, Fort Taber became operational. Its construction was overseen by Captain Henry Martyn Robert, who would later devise *Robert's Rules of Order*, which are still in use today.

Following the Civil War, more additions were made to the fort, which was renamed in 1898 for Lieutenant Colonel William Rodman, a New Bedford native who died in the Civil War. The two batteries next to the fort were constructed in 1899, and the installation remained operational through World Wars I and II before eventually being decommissioned and sold to the city; it is now a state park.

Many Civil War sites are imprinted with residual energy from those horrific battles. Gettysburg, for example, is considered by many to be the most haunted site in the world. The brutality of the dawn of modern warfare, combined with the emotional turmoil of fighting a war against one's own countrymen, made the psychic scars of the conflict worse than any other before or since. It's not unimaginable that even a small degree of those feelings have also imprinted themselves on the fort at Clark's Point.

As with most military haunts, phantom gunfire is frequently reported. Although the main facility of the fort is boarded up, there are a few spots where you can peer through worn-away stone; often, ghostly soldiers are seen patrolling the inside. The batteries feature a number of former storerooms that are now open and empty, and visitors at night have seen shadow figures darting among those storerooms, walking along the main structure's roof or seen in the lighthouse at the top of the fort.

There is also a Tiger tank from World War II on display outside the Fort Taber–Fort Rodman Military Museum, and at least one witness has reported seeing the apparition of a mechanic checking out the tank.

Seamen's Bethel

New Bedford of the early 1800s featured a unique dichotomy. There were still the remnants of the Puritans and Quakers who had originally settled the SouthCoast, frequently crossing paths with the rough-and-tumble lot that comprised the crews of the whaling vessels that sailed out of the harbor. Especially along the waterfront, there was a seedy underbelly to the Whaling

City that caused many residents to worry about the eternal souls of the whalers and sailors.

One group came together in 1830 as the New Bedford Port Society and was "dedicated to the moral and religious improvement of Seamen." In early 1831, they constructed a chapel with the intention of making it nondenominational but open to every sailor in order to worship and pray before heading out to sea. The Seamen's Bethel opened in May of 1832 and was made famous as the Whaleman's Chapel in Melville's *Moby Dick* in 1851.

Thirty-one black-framed cenotaphs adorn the chapel walls, representative of those men and ships lost at sea. There are still services held today to pray for the souls of those who never sailed home and perished in Davy Jones's Locker.

Melville wrote a famous scene in which a clergyman gives a hellfire-and-brimstone sermon on a pulpit that looks like the bow of a whaling vessel. However, that was a bit of creative license on his part; no such

This pulpit was inspired by *Moby Dick* and constructed in 1961. Does a ghostly clergyman offer his spectral sermons from its bow?

The Seamen's Bethel welcomes all beliefs, including belief in the paranormal.

pulpit existed. When the 1956 film version of the book, starring Gregory Peck, introduced a whole new generation to the story of the great white whale, tourism increased at the Seamen's Bethel yet most remained disappointed in not seeing the peculiar pulpit as described by Melville; in 1961, one was built, and it remains one of the most enduring images from the Bethel.

Melville visited Seamen's Bethel in 1840 while the seeds of *Moby Dick* were fertilizing in his mind, and the spot where he sat is immortalized with an inscription. Fans of his work often come here to see the spot and soak up the historic atmosphere within its walls—but they're not prepared for the spirit that may greet them.

The ghost of a former clergyman who served at Seaman's Bethel is said to roam the chapel, and his footsteps can be heard on the creaking wooden floor. The legend says that he was distraught over being unable to get the rowdy whalemen to see the error of their wicked ways and beg for the Lord's forgiveness, so he committed the ultimate sin and killed himself in the chapel itself, most likely by hanging. He hoped to make the people of the waterfront realize what true sin is, and that his death would make them repent. Modern reports say that those who enter the chapel and are disrespectful of it or God will feel the clergyman's wrath.

The Beast of Brooklawn Park

Located in the city's north end, Brooklawn Park features picturesque running and walking trails and is the home to youth baseball and softball leagues. It's a relaxing spot in the middle of the hustle and bustle of the city, but it's also the home to a mysterious creature that was seen in the late 1960s.

Witnesses described a manlike creature with hoofed feet running through the park and emitting a high-pitched laugh. They described as a real flesh-and-blood being, one that would stop and stare at park patrons before dashing off again.

Sightings seemed to have dropped off after the initial rash around 1968, but many who heard the stories back then still won't visit the park at night.

The Ghost that Got Away

The *Charles W. Morgan* now resides in the seaport of Mystic, Connecticut, but the whaling ship and the ghost that haunts it originally belonged in New Bedford.

Built in the city and launched from its harbor in 1841, the *Morgan* made over thirty-seven whaling voyages in eighty years of service. It eventually fell into disrepair, however, and was moved to a private residence in Dartmouth until it sailed to Mystic in 1941 to begin extensive restoration.

The *Morgan* is now one of the top tourist attractions at Mystic Seaport and is said to be inhabited by the spirit of Gerald, a nineteenth-century seaman who still works on the ship as he did more than one hundred years ago.

The initial investigation was done by the Rhode Island Paranormal Research Group, under the direction of Dr. Andrew Laird, after receiving numerous reports about spirit activity on the *Morgan* through the years. When the group received three similar reports from three different groups that described an encounter with a spirit aboard the ship, it decided to investigate.

Aboard the ship, Laird saw the apparition of Gerald, marking only the second time in his twenty-plus years of investigating the paranormal that he saw an actual ghost. Gerald's presence may have been tied into the fact that the *Morgan* was about to undergo an extensive restoration of the main hull that should be completed soon. The project, estimated to cost around $3.5 million, involved replacing the 30 percent of original timber still on the ship, which falls below the waterline. It was replaced by new live oak, including some two hundred trees donated from along the Mississippi coast that were uprooted in Hurricane Katrina—which, naturally, could bring some of their own ghosts with them as well.

Even now, nearly seventy years after the *Morgan* left New Bedford, its residents still call for Mystic to return the ship to its native port. Maybe then, Gerald can return home as well.

Lakeville and Freetown

In 1659, English settlers paid the sum of "20 coats, two rugs, two iron pots, two kettles, a little kettle, eight pairs of shoes, six pair of stockings, one dozen hoes, one dozen hatchets and two yards of broadcloth" to Massasoit for what was known as Ye Freeman's Purchase, a large tract of land that would eventually split into Fall River and Freetown, including the villages of East Freetown and Assonet (an Indian word to describe its rocky geography). It was the last land purchase made from the Wampanoags before the outbreak of King Philip's War.

Included in the deal was "a debt satisfied to John Barnes," which allegedly was for a large alcohol tab Massasoit had racked up in Barnes's tavern.

An interesting note regarding Freetown history: In 1699, the town voted to erect a meetinghouse to comply with the law of the colony, but it wasn't completed until 1713. It took even longer to find a clergyman to serve the town because they were more liberal in their beliefs and couldn't agree on who would suit the congregation as a whole. It wasn't until 1747 that they finally agreed on someone, and even then they forced him to sign a contract that stated that the town wouldn't pay his salary and, instead, he'd have to live on donations.

Lakeville, meanwhile, was part of the Middleboro settlement all the way until it was incorporated as its own separate town in 1853 and named for the large ponds found throughout.

Assawompset Pond

Assawompset Pond in Lakeville has the distinction of being the site where King Philip's War began. It was here that Metacom's men supposedly murdered John Sassamon and stowed his body under the pond's ice.

For that reason alone, we can deduce that the spectral Wampanoag seen walking along its shores and even atop its waves is Sassamon himself, but the pond has even deeper roots to his people that extend for thousands of years before the English ever stepped foot near it.

Assawompset is Wampanoag for "place of the white stones," which could be a reference to the quartz that is found in abundance throughout the area, the same mineral that records energy and is a factor in paranormal activity. The Indians would summer at Betty's Neck, find these stones and use them in their medicine rituals.

The pond is also a major component in one of the Wampanoag's greatest mythological tales. Maushop, a giant from ancient times who is sort of the

Lakeville's Assawompset Pond is the site where King Philip's War essentially began and its haunted history lives on.

tribe's creator god, was beloved by the Wampanoags. This brought great anger to the Pukwudgies (puck-wudge-ee), small troll-like creatures who were known as tricksters to the Wampanoag people.

According to Christopher Balzano on his Massachusetts Paranormal Crossroads website:

> *Standing between two and three feet tall, the Pukwudgie looks much like our modern idea of a troll. His features mirror those of the Native American in the area, but the nose, fingers and ears are enlarged and the skin is described as being grey and or washed-out, smooth and at times has been known to glow.*
>
> *What makes these monsters dangerous is the multitude of magical abilities they use to torment and manipulate people. They can appear and disappear at will and are said to be able to transform into other animals. They have possession of magical, poison arrows that can kill and can create fire at will. They seem to often be related to a tall dark figure, often referred to in modern times to shadow people. In turn the Pukwudgies control Tei-Pai-Wankas, which are believed to be the souls of Native Americans they have killed. They use these lights to entice new victims in the woods so they may kidnap or kill them. In European folklore these balls of energy are known as Will-o-the-Wisps and are said to accompany many paranormal occurrences. Modern paranormal investigators call them orbs, and catching one on film is the gold standard of field research.*

At the behest of his wife, Quant, Maushop rid his people of the Pukwudgies by shaking them and throwing them to the farthest reaches of civilization. However, they regrouped and returned, this time with far more evil intentions. Soon, they were kidnapping children and burning down homes, and in some cases killing the Wampanoag people. Maushop tried to have his five sons kill all the Pukwudgies, but the little demons overpowered each of them. Finally, Maushop tried to do the job himself, but they led him into the waters of Assawompset Pond and attacked him with their poison arrows.

One version of the myth suggests they killed Maushop, while another says that he grew despondent over the death of his sons and simply gave up the fight. Either way, it signaled the end of Maushop in Wampanoag lore, but it was only the beginning of the legend of the Pukwudgie. They are still reported today—mostly in the Freetown State Forest, discussed later in this chapter—and Balzano actively documents Pukwudgie sightings on his website and in his books.

While the spirit seen haunting Assawompset Pond is more likely Metacom or John Sassamon, it could also be the final resting place of the great Maushop. Only the Pukwudgies know for sure.

Lakeville Hospital

Just down the road from Assawompset Pond is the site of the former Lakeville Hospital, which originally opened as the Lakeville State Sanatorium in 1910 to treat those infected with tuberculosis.

Unlike the physically imposing insane asylums in Danvers and Taunton that were designed by Thomas Kirkbride, the Lakeville "San" was designed by John A. Fox to feature open-air verandas, as fresh air exposure was thought to alleviate the symptoms of TB and create a more homelike atmosphere.

Lakeville Hospital will soon be demolished, but don't expect its ghosts to go easily.

Still, abuse of patients did occur with frequency, including blasting cold water in the faces of patients in body casts or shoving their faces in their food. As TB waned in the second half of the twentieth century, the San was renamed Lakeville Hospital and turned to more general care before eventually becoming a long-term care facility until it closed for good in 1991.

Since then, the buildings have stood abandoned but guarded. Unlike other former hospitals and asylums that have become a haven for paranormal investigators and legend trippers alike, Lakeville has round-the-clock security to ward off those who attempt to trespass.

After it closed, the town sold the property for commercial development, and there were plans to demolish it in 2003. However, it still stands as of this writing, another example of how the ghosts might just be standing in the way of progress.

Many people who have walked by the hospital have reported hearing screams coming from the inside—but even creepier are the reports of the laughter of children. There was a children's ward in the old sanatorium, and the front building that was erected in the 1960s had a children's wing on the third floor. There are also rumors that some of the children who perished from tuberculosis in the early part of the twentieth century were buried in unmarked graves somewhere on the property, but a project manager for the site found no records of any burials in state documentation.

One paranormal investigator who has had the opportunity to investigate haunts all over the country told me Lakeville Hospital still remains his holy grail. His mother worked there before it closed, and she told him that even then, the staff would whisper about the ghostly children on the third floor who would throw open doors and bang on the windows, as if they were trying to escape.

Royal Wampanoag Cemetery

As pointed out on the website HauntedLakeville.com, the town of Lakeville has nearly one cemetery per square mile of land—twenty-eight in all. While many of them are family plots from the early days in the town's history, there is only one that can claim to be truly royal.

The Royal Wampanoag Cemetery sits on an isolated stretch of Route 105 on the shores of Little Quitticas Pond. In all, there are only a little

The descendents of Massasoit are buried in the Royal Wampanoag Cemetery in Lakeville.

more than twenty graves in the cemetery, each one a Native American and many believed to be relatives of Tispaquin, including Amie, Massasoit's only known daughter and Tispaquin's wife. Known as the Black Sachem for his darker skin tone, Tispaquin was one of Metacom's trusted lieutenants. When Metacom surrendered and was killed, Tispaquin surrendered a few days later, after Benjamin Church gave his word that his life would be spared. The promise was not kept, however.

Most of the graves are simple Wampanoag markers that descendents of the tribe still decorate and care for today. There are only a few graves with actual markers, including the grave of Lydia Tuspaquin (as the Tispaquin name was sometimes spelled), the last person buried in the cemetery back in 1812.

The most commonly reported phenomena here are phantom lights that dart about the graves. But a few travelers down Route 105 have also reported seeing a Wampanoag in traditional garb walking forlornly down the road, vanishing when he gets within site of the cemetery.

An example of an Indian grave at the Royal Wampanoag Cemetery.

A simple but effective crossing of faiths.

Paranormal investigators have also captured EVPs at the burial ground containing what sounds like Wampanoag words, although no translations could be found.

The Dark Woods

Simply put, the level of paranormal activity that occurs within the borders of the Freetown State Forest is astounding. It was enough for Balzano to write an entire book on the topic, called *Dark Woods: Cults, Crime and the Paranormal in the Freetown State Forest*. The title says it all.

In Balzano's expanded definition of the Bridgewater Triangle, the center of the vortex is not the Hockomock Swamp, but rather the nearly fifty-five hundred acres that comprise what is formally known as the Freetown–Fall River State Forest. Every type of paranormal activity imaginable has been reported there, from ghosts to UFOs to Bigfoot sightings. Balzano has even tracked stories about zombies, a witch who lives in the woods and haunts the dreams of young boys and, of course, the elusive Pukwudgies.

Yet as scary as the paranormal might be in the Freetown State Forest, what man has done there is far more heinous.

Because of its proximity to two cities and three major highways, the Freetown State Forest is used as both playground and dumping ground for the criminally minded.

In November 1978, fifteen-year-old Mary Lou Arruda was kidnapped and murdered, her body found tied to a tree in the Freetown State Forest. The main suspect was thirty-two-year-old James Kater, who was tried and convicted in 1979, but it took three subsequent retrials to make the verdict stick.

Part of the reason why doubt remained about Kater's guilt had to do with the high level of cult activity that takes place in the forest. While mutilated animals, altars, disfigured dolls and other such disturbing things had been found in the forest over the years, the cults remained mostly benign until the late 1970s and early 1980s.

That's when Carl Drew, a pimp working in the nearby city of Fall River, allegedly murdered several of his prostitutes and dumped their bodies in the forest. According to witnesses, Drew kept the women addicted to drugs and eventually lured them to his shack in the forest, where they would become human sacrifices for his cult. The case remains controversial to this day.

There have been other murders and attacks within the forest as well, and not all of it is cult related. In recent years, drug addicts have been a problem as well, using the isolation of the forest to ride out their high in peace. A Wampanoag ceremonial camp and cultural center was the victim of arson in 2009.

It's a chicken-and-the-egg argument when trying to figure out whether these dark events are influencing the paranormal aspects of the forest, or vice versa. But make no mistake, the negative energy there is extremely high and concentrated throughout its fifteen square miles.

The Assonet Ledge is one of the forest's most haunted spots. The predominant tale involves the Lady of the Ledge, who is said to be a Wampanoag princess who threw herself from atop the ledge when her father would not allow her to marry the white man she loved. That story, however, seems to be a modern concoction from those who don't know the history of the site. Although there may be spirits there that predate it, the ledge was part of a quarry that was operational in the early 1900s and provided much

The Assonet Ledge in the Freetown State Forest, where legends run as deep as the waters.

of the granite that was used to construct buildings in Fall River and even for work on some of the famed mansions in Newport, Rhode Island. What's interesting is that a number of the structures that have used this granite have hauntings attached to them as well.

Still, numerous reports of the lady have filtered in over the years, including a sighting by *Spooky Southcoast*'s Matt Moniz during his early adulthood. While out researching a flap of UFO sightings in the area of the ledge, he walked out from the road to the top of it and saw a woman in white standing near the edge. He turned to tell his companions about it, and when he turned around, she was gone.

Thinking she had jumped, he rushed to the edge but saw nothing in the water below. When recounting the incident to locals, they informed him he had seen the Lady of the Ledge. Prior to that, he had never heard of the legend.

According to Balzano's research, there have been at least eighteen confirmed suicides from the top of the ledge, as well as numerous others who have reported feeling suicidal with a strong desire to jump when at the top. There are also reports of ghostly figures plummeting from the top of it as well.

Mysterious lights have also been seen rising from the depths of the water below, yet unable to break the surface of it. There is speculation that these may be some type of alien craft—what's known as a USO, or unidentified submerged object—or they could be a form of the Pukwudgies of Wampanoag mythology.

Another site closely associated with the tribe is Profile Rock, which is formally known as Joshua's Mountain. The Wampanoags believed the natural formation jutting out of the side of the fifty-foot mound of granite resembled the face of Massasoit, and they revered the site. In subsequent years, however, it was privately owned until it was sold to the commonwealth and made into a state park in the early 1900s.

It is said that, from the top of Profile Rock, Wampanoag warriors could send smoke signals to Metacom back on his rocky "throne" on Mount Hope in Bristol, Rhode Island. Those same warriors are still reported atop the rock today, even in the daylight hours, and those traveling about the area often glimpse smoke coming from its quartz-covered peak.

It is also a reported hotbed for Bigfoot sightings as well, being the outermost portion of the Freetown State Forest before reaching the civilization of Assonet.

A 1963 image of Profile Rock clearly shows the face of Massasoit before erosion and graffiti took its toll. *Courtesy of Frank Wing.*

The forest itself is bisected by Copicut Road, which has its own ghostly legend, albeit one that is more story than substance. As the story goes, when driving down the road late at night, you'll see headlights in your rearview mirror and hear the blaring of a truck's air horn as the swerving vehicle tries to pass you. Once you finally do find a safe spot to pull over and let him pass, the truck vanishes.

The Mad Trucker of Copicut Road, as he's come to be known, is actually reported by very few people, yet the legend continues to grow. In what's become known as "legend tripping" (as featured in Jeff Belanger's books *Picture Yourself Legend Tripping* and *Weird Massachusetts*), sometimes it's more about the possibility of what might happen on a desolate dirt road than what actually does.

If This Rock Could Talk

Not far from the Freetown State Forest, in nearby Berkley, is Dighton Rock State Park. It is the site where a forty-ton boulder was discovered in colonial times, covered in strange writing and symbols that has yet to be determined. Some have speculated that it is an unknown Indian language, while others have deemed to it be of Norse or Portuguese origins. A few have even suggested that Phoenicians or Egyptians visited the area well before Christopher Columbus discovered the New World.

The Old Village House

One of the legends of Assonet that has gained legs in the paranormal community is that of the Old Village House. Whenever paranormal investigators come to this area and conduct online research of what they should check out, the story that always pops up about the Old Village House and how it is the site of one of Assonet's most heinous crimes.

As the story goes, it was in the early days of the town's existence, and the town's first selectman lived in the house with his family. He became angry with his teenage daughter for some reason, and a scuffle ensued in her second-story bedroom. The selectman inadvertently pushed his daughter out the bedroom window and she died when she struck the ground. In the years following her murder, her spirit has come to haunt the Old Village House, walking up and down its staircase with heavy footsteps, slamming doors closed and leaving scratch marks on the window of her bedroom.

It's a great story, and one that would certainly make an interesting investigation—if it existed.

The house in question may be what was known as the Old Homestead, which at one time was the oldest house in Assonet. There is no record, however, of any selectman pushing his daughter out a window. Believers of the tale will point out that in those days, such a story would be kept quiet for posterity, but you should be wary of this one.

The Assonet Inn

Another story that comes from the village is that of the Assonet Inn, and how it was a preferred rest stop for weary travelers during colonial times. In order to have a warm bed for the evening and to avoid possible harassment from area Indians, travelers would be more than happy to pay to spend the night at the inn along the shores of the Assonet River.

They'd check in—but they wouldn't check out.

Supposedly, some sinister people in the area—perhaps Indians, perhaps not—would rob these travelers, kill them and throw their bodies in the river. Thus, their spirits are said to linger around the river and attempt to warn others who try to stay at the inn.

It is another interesting tale, but one where the true history gets in the way of the good story. Actually, the Assonet Inn wasn't built until 1896, as a private residence for local Civil War hero major John Deane. It became an inn in 1940.

The Assonet Inn may bear the ghostly legends of a former Assonet tavern, the Green Dragon.

However, the Green Dragon Tavern did exist on the other side of the river from 1773 until the 1930s, when it was destroyed and replaced with the band shell that is still there today. Is it possible that this is a true story that was just transposed, over time, from one establishment to another?

One thing I am certain of—if you choose to dine or lodge at the Assonet Inn—you'll make it through your visit unscathed. And try the boneless fried chicken; it's to die for (pun intended).

DARTMOUTH AND WESTPORT

In early 1652, thirty-six settlers in the Massachusetts Bay Colony—including John Cooke, a passenger on the *Mayflower* in 1620—purchased what would become known as Dartmouth from the Wampanoags. Massasoit and his eldest son, Wamsutta, sold the lands to the English for the sum of "thirty yards of cloth, eight moose skins, fifteen axes, fifteen hoes, fifteen pairs of breeches, eight blankets, two kettles, one clock, two English pounds in Wampum, eight pair of shoes, one iron pot and ten shillings."

Not a bad price to pay for some of the most picturesque lands in the SouthCoast region, but, again, it was laughable to the Indians that anyone could actually own land.

About six months after the purchase, the Society of Friends (also known as the Quakers) left Plymouth to escape the strict religious views of the Puritans and worship as they saw fit. In November 1652, they settled Dartmouth, which was comprised of lands that were formerly known as Acushnea, Ponagansett and Coaksett.

In 1671, Richard Sisson and his family moved out to the Coaksett section of the settlement, also known as Acoaxet, in the area that would eventually secede from Dartmouth in 1787 and become Westport.

In modern times, each town is now known as a residential community, despite the bustling economic centers that have sprung along Route 6, which bisects each town as it heads west into Fall River. Both towns also feature sprawling farmland and gorgeous waterfronts as well.

The House that Hetty Bought

We learned of Hetty Green, the Witch of Wall Street and the World's Greatest Miser, when discussing the Millicent Library in Fairhaven. But Green had a more direct connection with Dartmouth, because when she died in 1916, her son Edward Howland Robinson Green inherited half of her $200 million fortune and freely spent her money, much to the benefit of the town and of science.

Green purchased Round Hill and erected a mansion that still stands today. Known as Colonel Green's Mansion—even though "Ned" Green had no military rank—it is now used as high-end condominiums in a private, gated community. But during Ned Green's time there, he allowed the Massachusetts Institute of Technology to conduct experiments such as atom-smashing at his mansion, and he also built his own radio station, WMAF, on the property and allowed MIT the use of his radio transmitters. MIT used the equipment to track polar expeditions and transatlantic zeppelin flights, while Green spent his time amassing one of the greatest stamp and coin collections of anyone at the time.

Ned Green also purchased the *Charles W. Morgan* and had it put on display at Round Hill, a nod to his family's roots in whaling. In 1933, he allowed physicist Robert J. Van de Graaff to conduct his electrical experiments at Round Hill, building the forty-foot-tall Van de Graaff generator that is still on display at the Museum of Science in Boston.

Green died in 1936, and, in 1948, his family donated Round Hill to MIT for continued experimentation and defense use. MIT eventually sold it off but not before constructing a giant radio telescope that would become known as the martini glass until it was demolished in 2007 to make room for new construction.

Considering the great deal of electrical equipment and experimentation at Round Hill, it's no surprise that visitors to its shores often reported seeing ghostly ships sailing through Buzzards Bay, apparently feeding off the energy generated from Colonel Green's mansion. What's more, ufologists recognize it as one of the East Coast's UFO hot spots. Since the erection of the radio telescope, there have been frequent reports of strange lights and mysterious objects in the sky. No doubt "Colonel" Green would have taken great delight in that knowledge.

Lurking in Lincoln Park

In 1894, the Union Street Railway Company was operating a line from New Bedford to Providence, Rhode Island. Disappointed with lagging sales on the weekends, the company purchased some lands around an old dance hall near the Dartmouth–Westport line and invested about $150,000 to build an amusement park that would be a destination point for city residents that was right along the Union Street line.

For nearly one hundred years, Lincoln Park was exactly what the company had hoped it would be, bringing families from miles around to enjoy its splendor. In 1946, the park added the Comet, a three-thousand-foot-long wooden roller coaster that featured top speeds of fifty-five miles per hour.

Baby boomers flocked to Lincoln Park in the summers of the 1950s, '60s and '70s, but by the mid-'80s, the park's attendance figures were in serious decline. Smaller, independently owned amusement parks like Lincoln Park or Rocky Point Park in nearby Warwick, Rhode Island, were often overlooked

All that remains of Lincoln Park in Dartmouth is the skeleton of the Comet.

by vacationers, who instead chose to make longer trips to larger theme parks outside of New England.

Safety issues began to plague the nearly century-old park as well. According to the website RideAccidents.com, a twenty-seven-year-old park employee was killed when he fell from atop the Comet on August 17, 1986. A year later on September 29, 1987, the Comet again was in the news when the brakes failed and one of the cars jackknifed on the track. The roller coaster never ran again, left in that position as the park closed permanently in December of that year.

Park owner Jay Hoffman sold off many of the rides and attractions to pay off debts, and what little remained of the park burned to the ground in subsequent fires around the now abandoned property. It soon became a haven for thrill-seeking teenagers and drug addicts, until they found out that even though the rides are gone, the ghosts remain.

The spirit of the park employee who fell from the Comet was often seen walking the tracks, making his usual daily inspection round. As the story goes,

The sign says No Trespassing, and so do the ghosts.

each time he got to the top of the steepest hill, he'd disappear—perhaps a residual haunt replaying to the point of the worker's fatal fall.

Other reports include the faint sounds of carousel music and the smell of Lincoln Park's famous clam cakes wafting through the air. These are common reports from abandoned amusement parks, and considering the high amount of energy exerted in these places—screaming, laughing, running children and strong feelings of joy, exuberance and adrenaline—it's no surprise that an imprint of that energy could remain behind.

While it's important to again note that no area should be investigated without permission, this is especially true of Lincoln Park. As tempting as it may be to hop the fence and climb what remains of the Comet, the wood has completely rotted through and it's only a matter of time until the rest of the ride crumbles to the ground. In addition, the land has been purchased for development into condominiums and a shopping center, and the neighbors keep a vigilant watch for trespassers.

Hell U

Colleges and universities are breeding grounds for urban legends. For some, such as Bridgewater State College or Stonehill College that are located within the Bridgewater Triangle, those legends are the product of actual paranormal activity. In the case of University of Massachusetts–Dartmouth (UMD), however, it's mostly just a good story.

Ask any student (and some of the faculty) at UMD, and they'll tell you about how the campus was designed by a man who was possessed by the devil; that he created it as an unholy temple to worship Satan; and who eventually was driven to leap off the campanile that stands in the center of the campus. Some legends even claim that he did it on June 6 sometime between the hours of 9:00 p.m. and 12:00 a.m., and, from that point on, whenever the calendar reaches the sixth of any month, his glowing spirit can be seen atop the tower between 9:00 and midnight.

The odd details of the campus design certainly don't help dispel this rumor, either. The infamous 666 benches are often the first thing incoming freshmen want to see. Three walking paths that cross the campus converge in front of the liberal arts and auditorium buildings in rounded alcoves with benches inside them. From a ground-level perspective, the design doesn't make much sense, but take a look from one of the upper floors and clearly

The University of Massachusetts–Dartmouth, where some believe the campus was designed by a devil worshipper.

see that the three paths and rounded alcoves spell out 666, the number of the beast. There are also six steps in each of the three staircases outside of them.

Other claims that have less validity are that the buildings are all in the shape of the number six (Google Earth easily dispels this notion); each staircase on the campus grounds contains either six or thirteen steps, with the six-stepped staircases always grouped in threes with each stair being six inches high; there are no clocks within the buildings so students won't realize when the clock has struck midnight; the campanile is a giant beacon broadcasting to demons around the world; the campanile is also supposed to represent a giant middle finger giving the salute to God; the buildings' roofs were made flat in order to accommodate flying cars in the future promised by Satan; and the concrete structures are designed to keep students feeling cold, anxious and desperate.

If you believe these stories, you'd think UMD was the second coming of Dana Barrett's apartment building from *Ghostbusters*, and that the architect was Ivo Shandor. So what is the truth? The campus was designed by Paul Rudolph, a student of the Brutalist movement that features sharply angled concrete structures as part of its general design. Rudolph also designed City

Hall in Boston and the J. Edgar Hoover FBI Building in Washington, D.C., and neither of those places is accused of being the gates of hell.

When I was a student at UMD in the mid- to late 1990s, I was already hearing tales about how the architect had leapt from the campanile. In actuality, Rudolph died of cancer in 1997, after years of exposure to asbestos.

The Spirits that Haunted the DeMello Family

While this book intentionally steers clear of hauntings of private residences, there is one intriguing SouthCoast case that has come to public light in recent years.

In the book *Our Demons, Our Forefathers: Ghostly Encounters in a Sleepy New England Town*, coauthors Thomas DeMello and Thomas Nickerson share their experiences growing up in Westport and as a Native American spirit with bad intentions plagued the DeMello family at two different residences within the town. The stories are so incredible that they may seem unbelievable—until you consider the reputations that both authors are putting on the line in telling their story. Nickerson is an English teacher at New Bedford High School, and DeMello is a police officer for the City of Fall River. As we all learned when we were children, if there are two kinds of people you can trust, they are teachers and police officers.

The Icehouse

The icehouse is located along the shores of North Watuppa Pond, which supplies Fall River with its drinking water. North Watuppa Pond drains into South Watuppa Pond, and the two are on the border of Westport and Fall River. The icehouse was built in 1864, and the stone building was used to keep chunks of ice from the frozen pond of the winter in order to provide blocks of ice for residents' iceboxes in the summer.

The rumor is that the icehouse burned in a fire, the result of arson while child laborers toiled inside and were unable to escape, but others say it merely crumbled after years of neglect, and the fires were part of the strange incidents that took place in subsequent years. Either way, it has developed a reputation not only for being haunted but also for being a spot in which rituals and animal mutilations are conducted for nefarious purposes. Reports of bloodstained walls and pentagrams drawn on the floor are also common.

If this type of negative activity is going on, the energy could be easily trapped by the remaining fieldstone within the structure. Perhaps that's why many of the ghost stories surrounding the icehouse feature angry spirits attempting to drive visitors away. There are even reports of large black dogs with red eyes—or hellhounds, as they are known in folklore—chasing people from the site.

The Slave House

In the late 1700s, there was a significant number of blacks living in Dartmouth. Part of the reason was because of its more tolerant Quaker attitude—in stark contrast to the Puritans—but also because of the proximity of Dartmouth and Westport to Newport, Rhode Island, the hub of the northern slave trade.

In 1780, seven of these black residents asked to be granted the right to vote. They were already tax-paying citizens and Revolutionary War veterans, and they felt they deserved the same rights as white men. Their petition was denied by the town; but in 1783, slavery was declared illegal in Massachusetts, and even if they couldn't vote, at least the black residents of Dartmouth were free—or so they thought.

According to legend, one sea captain living in the vicinity of what is now Cornell Road in Westport took exception to the government telling him whether he had the right to own slaves. Slaves were not only an integral part of his crew, but he also viewed them as inferior beings. Instead of allowing his slaves to become freemen, he instead murdered them by drowning each of them in a basin kept in his cellar. Subsequent residents of the property report phantom splashing sounds in the basement and say that any water left down there evaporates at a quickened pace, as if some unseen force wants to be rid of the water as a reminder of something horrible.

Now more than two hundred years later, the spirits of these slaves still roam the property where they died, unable to achieve freedom from the sea captain's grasp, even in death.

The House Next to White's

Approach any SouthCoast resident and ask them to name a nearby haunted location, and it's a sure thing that a good majority of them will mention, without a moment's hesitation, "the house next to White's."

What they are referring to is a rather nondescript home that was situated just to the east of White's of Westport, a landmark function facility along Route 6. Visible from the highway that leads from Westport into Fall River, it sat abandoned for many years as its legend continued to grow until it recently burned down.

Located near a cemetery, its haunted legend suggested the house had actually been built over a Native American burial ground that may have already been cursed before it had been desecrated by a white man's dwelling. It seems as though everyone in the area knows someone who used to live there and has a tale to tell about apparitions of Indians parading through the house, unseen hands gripping at them from under the bed or strange noises emitting from the house, even after the home was vacant.

Teenagers and thrill seekers who approached the house in its later years would often report a general heaviness surrounding the property, an oppressive and unwelcoming feeling that would strengthen as you got closer to the front door. Those brave enough to peek in its windows reported seeing macabre sights such as coffins lined up along a far wall.

In actuality, the home was vacant because it was purchased by a nearby funeral parlor as storage for their extra inventory. That may account for the coffins but not for the rest of the activity reported. The legend has grown to such proportions that, for many, it will always be known as the SouthCoast's most infamous haunted house.

FALL RIVER

Fall River has always had a bit of an identity problem. The city began as part of Ye Freeman's Purchase in 1659, originally a part of Freetown before breaking out on its own in 1803 under the name of Fall River, named for the Quequechan River that runs through it. *Quequechan*, in Wampanoag, means "falling river," as it has eight falls within its run to Mount Hope Bay.

However, in 1804, the town changed its name to Troy and would remain that way for the next thirty years, before reverting back to the Fall River name in 1834.

Until the textile boom of the early 1800s that would carry the city through almost to the twenty-first century, Fall River always struggled with who it was as a community. Located practically equidistant from both New Bedford and Providence, Rhode Island, it felt tugs from both sides. It wasn't until August 4, 1892, that the city had its defining moment, and that moment would eventually become known as the Fall River tragedy. Now, the city will be forever linked with Lizzie Borden, the young woman who allegedly took an ax and killed her father and stepmother.

Quequechan Club

Of course, Fall River is a place rich in history and culture and is a lot more than just a pair of grisly ax murders that still stand unsolved. A prime example of that is the Quequechan Club on North Main Street, within sight of Battleship Cove (a large collective of naval battleships and a maritime museum that remains one of Fall River's top tourist attractions) and just a stone's throw from the house where Lizzie—or someone else—changed the course of city history forever.

The Quequechan Club in Fall River once catered to the city's elite, but did it also have a seedy underbelly?

The Quequechan Club, or Q-Club, was organized by a group of nine men on November 22, 1894, and featured some of the most respected and wealthiest members of Fall River Society. They purchased the mansion on North Main, known then as the William Mason Estate, as their clubhouse. The house itself had been built in 1861. After extensive renovations within the Mason mansion, the club purchased Dr. Hubert Wilbur's adjacent property next door and opened it in 1920 as the Ladies' Annex. A bowling alley was built in the basement of the main clubhouse and is still in use today, home to the longest-existing bowling league on the East Coast.

Although extensive records were kept of members, not much is known about what actually went on at the club during its early days.

Dan Silva was already a longtime club member when he purchased it with two other members in 1999. He's since become the Quequechan's sole owner, and although he had some unusual experiences while conducting his own renovations on the property, he never considered it haunted until a paranormal team uncovered some rather convincing evidence.

Under Dan's ownership, the club has retained its elegance while becoming much more affordable for the average blue-collar citizen of Fall River. He built a casual sports pub in the basement, yet it still offers fine dining (with a tie and jacket required) in the main dining room. An electrician by trade, Dan is a straightforward guy and runs his club in much the same manner. Yet even he started to question his beliefs when sitting at the bar with a friend who claimed to see a woman in a Victorian dress walk by. While Dan didn't see it himself, his trust in his friend's word and the pale expression on his face convinced Dan that his friend had truly seen something.

When Eric LaVoie of DART approached him about possibly conducting a paranormal investigation there (Eric, like me, thinks activity can be found in historic buildings even if it hasn't been reported or experienced), Dan agreed, and Eric began to interview the staff about their experiences there. The kitchen staff spoke of a bell usually used to summon servers to pick up their orders that would often ring when nobody was near it. This is the type of bell a school teacher might have on their desk, which requires the pushing of a button at the top to activate the hammer on the inside of the bell.

Other activity was reported as well, and on a preliminary walk-through, Eric picked up other bits and pieces of activity before returning for a more thorough investigation a short time later. In addition to personal experiences and a few strange orbs of light, he captured EVPs with such claims as "call the doctor" (perhaps Dr. Wilbur from next door?), "stop it" and "get out of here." He also asked if a spirit was present that it make a knocking sound. Two distinct knocks were heard, and that was enough to convince Dan to allow further investigation.

Eric invited *Spooky Southcoast*, Luann Joly of Whaling City Ghosts, Andrew Lake of Greenville Paranormal Research and EVP researcher Mike Markowicz to join him in a subsequent investigation, which resulted in even more evidence. In addition to many more intriguing EVPs, we also got some solid evidence from a device known as a Shack Hack.

In the 1990s, an engineer named Frank Sumption began messing around with radios he believed would help him communicate with extraterrestrials and beings of a higher realm. Sumption told me that he didn't know why he built these devices, but he was compelled to do so. He later found out Thomas Edison had been working on a similar device that he called the Telephone to the Dead before he passed away. Although Frank mostly communicated with what he believes are alien beings, ghost researchers began using the device to talk to spirits.

Known as Frank's Boxes, the devices are essentially radios that sweep through all the frequencies without stopping on any particular one. The theory is that the spirit grabs whatever words are out there that it needs to express itself. The Shack Hack is a stripped-down version of a Frank's Box, made by removing the "mute" circuit from a thirty-dollar Radio Shack portable AM/FM radio. By cutting that circuit and pressing "seek," the radio will continue scanning through the frequencies without stopping when it receives a strong signal.

At the Quequechan Club, we brought the Shack Hack up to the third floor, which Dan was in the process of renovating into either offices or small rooms for lodging. The design of the room made us think that perhaps, at some point, the upper floor of the club had been used to entertain its male membership while the women were next door at the Ladies' Annex. The spirit that came through confirmed that suspicion, claiming to be Marie, a prostitute who was kept at the club for mobsters that came down from Providence.

During the investigation, we tried a few different tactics to draw more responses out of Marie. First, we had Luann, who is sensitive to spirits, stay on the third floor alone and communicate with the spirit in a kind and understanding way. Through both EVP and the Shack Hack, Marie was very open with Luann and spoke of abuse suffered at the hands of the men who kept her there.

Later, we shifted strategies and had Luann go downstairs while just the men remained on the third floor. We began speaking to Marie in a very direct and angry manner. We called her unmentionable names and told her she was worthless, to see if this approach would gather a stronger reaction from her. This is known as provoking the spirit, and while some consider it disrespectful, it can be very effective in getting paranormal activity to strengthen and become more overt.

Marie, though, simply made one last stand and then refused to say much more.

Cindy Bouchard, now the manager of the Wamsutta Club in New Bedford, worked in the same capacity at the Quequechan Club prior to Dan Silva taking ownership. She reported feeling a presence on that third floor, to the point where she would knock and announce herself before entering.

She shared the following experience in an email:

I worked at the Q-Club from 1988 to 1996. Here are several things that I remember that could be viewed as strange or paranormal. I always remember the feeling that I would get when I went upstairs to the back half of the third floor. It was used to hold extra dishes and a few supplies. We didn't store much up there because no one would go up there. I actually would knock on the door and announce myself before going in. I always felt a presence there.

We were closed on Saturdays and we had an outside catering job for a member's daughter's wedding. The entire staff was there and we loaded the trucks. I was the last one out and set the alarm. When we left the catering job to return to the club I was the first to arrive so that I could shut the alarm off. When I opened the door and turned on the light I saw a figure run up the stairs. I was startled and turned off the alarm. I walked over to the staircase and noticed an afghan lying on the stairs. I looked up but didn't go. The chef came in with the staff behind him so I told him about it. He decided to go upstairs to check it out. He of course didn't find anything. I folded the afghan and put it on the shelf in the ladies room. We cleaned up, put everything away and left. On Monday I returned and the afghan was gone.

We served lunch from 11:30 to 2:00 PM everyday. We would hear pool balls dropping on the hard wood floors upstairs. It was always at lunchtime. We would check and there were no pool balls on the floor and no one was ever there.

One Saturday I was at the club doing some work. The maintenance man was working outside doing some landscaping. We were the only ones there. He came into my office and said that he was done and was going upstairs to take a shower before he left. I told him not to lock up because I would be working for awhile. He said fine and left to go upstairs. A few minutes later he came into my office very upset and told me that he didn't think that I was funny. I asked him what he was talking about. He said that when he got upstairs the shower was already on and there was shaving cream on the mirror that said "Get Out". I tried to say that it wasn't me but he wouldn't listen and walked away. I went upstairs to check for myself and there was nothing there. No shaving cream and the shower wasn't on. I decided to go home too.

Research into the Q-Club has yet to determine who this Marie might have been, and if these claims of a third-floor bordello have any merit. The Quequechan Club of today, however, is a fine establishment of which this writer later became a card-carrying member.

Oak Grove Cemetery

Earlier in this book, we mentioned that most cemeteries don't get much attention from seasoned paranormal investigators. Oak Grove Cemetery in Fall River is one of the rare exceptions.

Oak Grove is the final resting spot of the Borden family and is a frequent stop for those who visit Fall River to investigate the murder case. A tall stone pillar marks the graves of Lizzie's father, Andrew Borden, his first wife (and Lizzie's mother), Sarah, and second wife, Abby. Lizzie, meanwhile, lay under a small, simple stone that reads "Lizbeth," with none of the pomp or ornate style she became accustomed to later in her life.

Since Andrew and Abby were first interred at Oak Grove, there have been constant claims about their spirits lurking about the cemetery. Many people who visit the graves report getting sick to their stomachs and are overwhelmed with feelings of dread and paranoia. There are also reports of strange lights flitting about, and even screams that come from beneath that great stone pillar.

In 1992, during the centennial observance of the crime, forensic scientist James E. Starrs wanted to exhume Andrew and Abby to further examine their wounds and cause of death. His request was denied, and the bodies of Andrew and Abby remain six feet below the surface of Oak Grove Cemetery. The question is—where are their souls?

THE LIZZIE BORDEN BED & BREAKFAST: THE SOUTHCOAST'S MOST FAMOUS HAUNT

We've already established that you can't separate Fall River from the tragedy of the Borden murders, when someone brutally murdered banker and merchant Andrew Borden and his second wife, Abby Durfee Gray Borden, with a hatchet on the morning of August 4, 1892. Even now, 118 years later (as of this writing), the stain on the city is just as fresh as it was then.

Let us start this discussion by stating that, for the record, Lizzie Borden was acquitted by a jury of her peers for the murders on June 20, 1893. As far

The Lizzie Borden Bed & Breakfast in Fall River is the SouthCoast's most haunted house.

as the Commonwealth of Massachusetts is concerned, there was reasonable doubt that Lizzie committed this heinous crime. Do I think she did it? Well, I often waver in that. I think she certainly had the motive—even beyond what we'll discuss later in this chapter.

Lizzie Borden was a thirty-two-year-old spinster still living at home at the time of the murders. She longed for the life that her father's wealth could afford her family, yet in his miserly ways he chose not to provide. She loathed her stepmother, Abby, and was jealous of anything her father would give to her, whom Lizzie and older sister Emma viewed as an outsider even after more than a decade of living with her.

Lizzie Andrew Borden—spinster, socialite, accused murderer and ghost? *Courtesy of Stefani Koorey.*

Andrew Borden was a hard man, one who viewed money and the accumulation of it above all else. His home at 92 Second Street was far more modest than it needed to be. Andrew could be living on the Hill with the rest of the Bordens and Fall River's upper class, but instead he chose to remain "down below." He would not have indoor plumbing installed in his home, forcing his family to use chamber pots and an outhouse, like common peasants. He would often purchase nearly expired food in order to save a few pennies, and indeed, breakfast on the morning of his death included rancid mutton stew.

Abby, from all accounts, did the best she could with the family she married into. While not particularly loving, she wasn't exactly abusive

The Borden House in 1892. *Courtesy of Stefani Koorey.*

either. But as is often the case with children who lose a parent to an untimely death, the "steppie" could never replace the parent lost.

Increasing arguments over money and one piece of property in particular is believed to be at the root of the tension that existed in the Borden household on that warm August morning.

Since this book is about the ghosts and not about solving what was the crime of the nineteenth century, we'll leave it at that. In order to give the reader a more accurate view of what went down in the Borden house on that particular day, I've included a modified timeline from the *Tattered Fabric* blog of Borden expert Faye Musselman (phayemuss.wordpress.com) that is an excellent Lizzie Borden resource. In addition, Musselman has acquired some interesting documents that breathe new life into the Borden case, which she shared publicly for the first time on the July 31, 2010 edition of *Spooky Southcoast* and which we will recount later in this chapter.

Timeline of the Borden Murders

August 3, 1892   **The day before the murders**

8:00 a.m.   Abby goes across street to Dr. Seabury Bowen; tells him she fears she's been poisoned.

About 9:00   Dr. Bowen crosses street to check on the Bordens; Lizzie dashes upstairs; Andrew rebuffs his unsolicited visit.

10:00 to 11:30   Lizzie attempts to buy prussic acid from Eli Bence at Smith's Pharmacy on Columbia Street.

1:30 p.m.   John Morse, uncle to Lizzie and brother of Andrew's first wife, Sarah, walks from the train station and arrives at the Borden house; Abby lets him in front door.

2:00 to 4:00   Morse and Andrew talk in sitting room; Lizzie hears the conversation. There is speculation that Andrew is discussing with Morse a land transfer deal. The rumor is that Andrew is going to give a piece of property that Lizzie and Emma desire to Abby, and the transfer will happen soon. Morse then leaves on a trip to nearby Swansea.

7:00   Lizzie visits Alice Russell in the early evening, stating her fear "something will happen" to her father.

8:45   Morse returns from Swansea, talks in sitting room with Andrew and Abby.

9:00   Lizzie returns from Alice Russell's, locks front door and goes upstairs to her room without speaking to father or uncle.

9:15   Abby Borden retires to bed.
10:00   Andrew and Morse retire to bed.

August 4, 1892   **The day of the murders** (Note: Times given are based on various testimonies taken primarily from the Preliminary Hearing held August 25 to September 1, 1892, and are approximated as close as possible).

6:15 a.m.   Maid Bridget Sullivan goes downstairs, gets coal and wood in cellar to start a fire in the kitchen stove and takes in milk.

6:20	Morse goes downstairs to the sitting room.
6:30	Abby comes downstairs and gives orders for breakfast to Bridget
6:40 to 6:50	Andrew goes downstairs, empties slops, picks up pears and goes to the barn.
6:45	Bridget opens side (back) door for the iceman.
7:00	The Bordens and Morse have breakfast in dining room. Lizzie is still upstairs.
7:45 to 8:45	Morse and Andrew talk in sitting room; Abby sits with them a short while before she begins to dust.
8:45	Andrew lets Morse out the side door and invites him back for dinner.
8:45 to 8:50	Lizzie comes down and enters kitchen.
8:45 to 9:00	Abby tells Bridget to wash windows, inside and out. Bridget goes outside to vomit. Andrew leaves the house. Bridget returns; she does not see Lizzie or Andrew but sees Abby dusting in dining room.
9:00	Abby goes up to guest room.
9:00 to 9:30	Bridget cleans away breakfast dishes in kitchen. Bridget gets brush from cellar to wash the windows Lizzie appears at back door as Bridget goes towards barn; Bridget tells Lizzie she does not need to lock the door.
9:15 to 9:45	Morse arrives at 4 Weybosset Street to visit his niece and nephew.
9:30	Abraham G. Hart, treasurer of Union Savings Bank, talks to Andrew at the bank.
9:30 to 10:00	Abby Borden dies from blows to the head with a sharp instrument.
9:30 to 10:05	Andrew visits banks.
9:45	John P. Burrill, cashier, talks to Andrew at National Union Bank.
9:50 to 10:00	Andrew deposits Troy Mill check with Everett Cook at First National Bank; talks with William Carr.
9:30 to 10:20	Bridget washes outside windows, stops to talk to "Kelly girl" at the south fence.

10:00 to 10:30	Mrs. Churchill sees Bridget outside washing northeast windows.
10:20	Bridget reenters house from the side door, commences to wash inside windows.
10:30 to 10:40	Mrs. Kelly observes Andrew going to his front door. Andrew Borden can't get in the side door and fumbles with key at front door; he is let in by Bridget. Bridget hears Lizzie laugh on the stairs as she says "pshaw," fumbling with inside triple locks.
10:35 to 10:45	Bridget sees Lizzie go into dining room and speak in a low manner to her father.
10:45	Mark Chase, residing over Wade's store, sees a man at the Borden fence taking pears.
10:45 to 10:55	Lizzie puts an ironing board on the dining room table as Bridget finishes the last window in the dining room. Lizzie asks Bridget in the kitchen if she's going out; Lizzie tells her of note to Abby and a sale at Sargeant's.
10:50 to 10:55	Mark Chase observes a man with an open buggy parked just beyond tree in front of the Borden house.
10:55	Bridget heads upstairs to her room to lie down.
10:55 to 10:58	Bridget goes up to her room; lies down on her bed.
10:55 to 11:00	Andrew Borden dies from blows to the head with a sharp instrument.
11:00	Bridget hears City Hall clock chime.
11:05 to 11:10	Hyman Lubinsky drives his cart past the Borden house.
About 11:10	Lizzie hollers to Bridget to come down, saying "someone has killed Father."
11:10 to 11:12	Lizzie sends Bridget to get Dr. Bowen.
11:10 to 11:13	Bridget rushes back across street from the Bowens', telling Lizzie he's not home. Lizzie asks Bridget if she knows where Alice Russell lives and tells her to go get her. Mrs. Churchill observes Bridget crossing street, notices a distressed Lizzie and calls out to Lizzie; she tells him "someone has murdered Father."
11:10 to 11:14	Mrs. Churchill goes to the side door, speaks briefly to Lizzie and then crosses the street, looking for a doctor.

11:16 to 11:20	Dr. Bowen pulls up in his carriage and is met by his wife, and they rush over to Bordens.
	John Cunningham checks outside cellar door in the Borden back yard and finds it locked.
11:20 to 11:22	Officer Allen checks the front door and notes it bolted from inside; he also checks the closets in the dining room and kitchen.
11:20	Morse departs Daniel Emery's on Weybosset Street and takes a streetcar back to the Bordens.
11:23 to 11:30	Lizzie asks to check for Mrs. Borden; Bridget and Mrs. Churchill go upstairs and discover body.
11:35 to 11:40	Officer Doherty questions Lizzie, who tells him she heard a "scraping" noise.
11:35 to 11:45	Morse arrives at the Borden house and goes first to the back yard.
11:45	Morse talks to Officer Sawyer at the side door, yet Morse later testifies he heard of murders from Bridget.
11:45 to 11:50	Morse sees Andrew's body; then he goes upstairs and sees Abby's body.
11:50	Morse speaks to Lizzie as she lies on lounge in dining room.
11:50	Morse goes out to the back yard and stays outside most of the afternoon.
11:50 am to noon	Assistant Marshal Fleet arrives, sees the bodies and talks to Lizzie in her room with Reverend Buck; Lizzie says "she's not my mother, she's my stepmother."
	Officers Doherty, Fleet and Medley accompany Bridget to cellar, where she shows them a hatchet in a box on the shelf.
5:00 p.m.	Emma arrives in Fall River.
8:45	Officer Joseph Hyde, observing from a northwest outside window, sees Lizzie and Alice go down to the cellar.

Haunt or Hoax?

In 1996, the former Borden home became a bed and breakfast under the ownership of Martha McGinn. Originally belonging to her grandfather, John McGinn, there were no reports of paranormal activity during its time as the McGinn's private residence. However, once the house became open to the public, strange things began happening—enough that the television series *Unsolved Mysteries* paid a trip to Fall River to document some of the ghostly incidents.

While all of this seemed interesting to a paranormalphile such as me, I took much of it in stride. Growing up, my mother and her sisters were deeply interested in the Borden case, so I knew its grisly details. I figured now that the house was a commercial venture, the ghosts were simply marketing.

Those thoughts were even more solidified after a 2005 episode of *Ghost Hunters* in which TAPS investigated the house and no activity was captured. Investigator Steve Gonsalves famously quipped, "Any place with a gift shop can't be haunted," and for the moment, I agreed. Lee-ann Wilber, who along with Donald Woods had purchased the property from the Martha McGinn, was now claiming to have experiences. I remained skeptical.

Even upon my first visit in June 2006, I was convinced the haunt existed solely in people's minds, that they were tripping on the legend instead of experience the paranormal. I was led on a tour along with *Spooky Southcoast* cohost Matt Costa by Eleanor Thibeault, the tour guide who had shared her experiences on *Unsolved Mysteries*. As she recounted those experiences to us, I got the feeling that she did believe she experienced something, but I wasn't convinced it was anything paranormal.

All that changed in October 2006.

Can You Move My Legs?

One of our radio show's loyal listeners had traveled from California to the East Coast to spend her birthday exploring some of the very locations we talk about on the air each week. She was celebrating her birthday at the Lizzie Borden Bed & Breakfast, having rented the place out for a night of uninterrupted, untainted investigation. We were invited to join along and jumped at the chance.

During the course of the night, it became clear that there was some sort of presence lurking about. Everyone felt it, and many of us were about as psychic as a brick. I tempted fate by lying in the exact spots where Andrew and Abby's mutilated bodies were found—nothing. I called out for the spirits to come and get me—still nothing. It wasn't until I decided to take a break that something occurred.

The house consists of eight guest rooms spread over the top two floors, with the ground floor consisting of a sitting room, a parlor, a dining room and a kitchen. Each guest room is named after someone either from the Borden family or pertaining to the case. On the third floor is two rooms named for the lawyers who tried the case; the Hosea Knowlton Room is commonly referred to as the "chimney room" because of the chimney that bisects it. It was in this room that I decided to lie across the bed, perpendicular to the way one would normally lie, and rest for a few moments.

Immediately I felt a tingle come over my hands, which I had folded across my chest. A cold began to envelop me. I called out to the rest of the investigators, who were in the next room and then came and verified the cold spot with digital thermometers. Touching my hands, they could feel the electricity causing them to tingle.

I asked aloud that if anything was in the room and if so, could it do something to let me know it was there? Almost immediately, I felt two unseen hands grab my ankles and begin slowly lifting my legs up off the side of the bed. Observers could actually see where the invisible hands were pinching the tops of my sneakers. After a time, it let my feet down, and we were able to re-create the phenomena with others both that night and repeatedly since. Of course, that was only my introduction to the spirits of the Borden house.

The Kids from Next Door

In that same room, there is a chest full of small toys. If the trunk is left open (and some say, the closet door is left ajar as well), when returning to the room you will find the toys spread out over the floor, as if a child had been playing with them. These are believed to be the spirits of two children who were murdered next door. An article given to me by Wilber from a newspaper clipping at the time of the trial specifically mentions that in the house next door, a relative of the Bordens who shared the same surname "had thrown her three young children in a cistern to drown and afterward jumped in and died with them. She endeavored to get her fourth child in with the rest, but the little one escaped." Only two of those children have been detected by mediums visiting the Borden house, and they claim their names are Sally and James.

Michael, Did You Move the Camera?

Another spirit who may be in that room is Michael, the former caretaker. When Wilber and Woods bought the house, they couldn't afford to keep him on so he was let go. Shortly after, he died in a fire. His presence has been documented by Elizabeth Nowicki, the house psychic, who has communicated with him many times. In fact, during the course of one of our investigations, Nowicki was speaking with Michael when an infrared camera that Matt Moniz had placed on the trunk in the room moved completely on its own. After being reset, it did the exact same thing a few moments later. Repeated attempts to try and make it move in the same manner by tugging on the cable or stomping on the floor failed to achieve the same result. You can view it for yourself on the *Spooky Southcoast* page on YouTube and see what you think.

As time went on, the two Matts and I became friends with Wilber and were afforded the opportunity to investigate the Lizzie Borden Bed & Breakfast on a frequent basis. By continually studying the phenomena at one specific location, we're able to chart how it changes, whether it gets stronger or weaker or whether it trends toward one particular form of evidence or another. For example, the leg-lifting went on for quite some time, but now it rarely happens. EVPs were once a frequent capture, but now it seems as though we're hearing more noises with our own ears rather than on recorded media. And Lee-ann can't be thanked enough for her patience with our random visits and all-nighters. Not only is she a good friend to us, but she's a good friend to paranormal research.

We've brought numerous other investigators with us, each with their own specializations and unique abilities and techniques. The house almost never fails to impress, so much so that when we're contacted by local media outlets, which usually happens every Halloween, we recommend they join us for a night with Lizzie and the family.

"But I'm a Good Daughter"

One night in August 2007, a local magazine writer tagged along on an investigation between *Spooky Southcoast* and Whaling City Ghosts. The writer was a true skeptic and wanted to experience something monumental. At Lizzie's, that wouldn't take long.

For some reason, on that particular night, the spirits in the house were exceptionally interactive. When Liz Nowicki was hanging with us for a bit, she sensed Andrew Borden's presence while we were in the Morse Room, which is the room in which Abby Borden was killed.

Now, Andrew and I have never liked each other, for reasons we'll get into later. Let's just say I know his secret, and I'm not afraid to share. Usually, I'm the object of his ire, but on this particular night he went after Liz. His unseen form scratched at her, and we could see those scratches develop on

Abby Borden was found in the upstairs bedroom, killed by nineteen blows to the head with an ax. *Courtesy of Stefani Koorey.*

The room is now known as the John Morse Room.

her arms and shoulders (it was summer and she was wearing a tank top) without anyone touching her. Soon, they progressed to the point of welts. I yelled out, "Leave her alone, Andrew! Pick on someone your own size! I won't even fight back!" as I stood near the wall in the very spot were Abby's body was discovered and put both my arms behind my head, elbows sticking out in front of me. Suddenly I felt two invisible hands push down firmly on my elbows and start pushing me up against the wall. I tried to push back, but I found it very hard to do so. I stood there wrestling with something none of us could see for a good two or three minutes, until he finally pinned me against the wall.

It wasn't the first time I'd been accosted by the spirits there. Previously, I had been choked while trying to stop a spirit from pinching a young boy (you know how when your aunt pinches your cheek too tight? Imagine seeing that happening to a kid, but with no hand there) and another time, I was pushed on the stairs exiting the basement to the backyard.

Later in our night with the journalist, we were all discussing what to do next while gathered in Lizzie's bedroom. With our recorders running, we were simply having a conversation, not conducting a formal EVP session. Yet in the recording, you can hear, very loudly and distinctly, a female voice with a Victorian-era accent exclaim "but I'm a good daughter!" We've come to believe this is the actual voice of Lizzie Borden, either proclaiming her innocence or hoping we won't judge her based on that one morning of indiscretion in August 1892. There is clear desperation in her voice.

During that same investigation, we also encountered two memorable EVPs while formally conducting a session. In one, we're in the Knowlton room, and I'm asking the spirit to lift my legs again. A whispery voice then states directly into the recorder's microphone "Why don't you go (expletive) yourself?" In the same session, I'm speaking to the other investigators and the same voices calls me an "a—hole."

Like I said, they don't like me very much.

The Flying Picture

Every once in a while, though, the ghosts in the house turn their attention to someone else. That's what happened one night when Matt Moniz was hanging out in the parlor, having a conversation with a few other guests while a tour was going on elsewhere in the house.

During the course of their discussion, a silver picture frame lifted up off an end table to about Matt's eye level, slowly rolled end over end in midair, stopped and then flew across the room as if it was thrown by a major-league ace.

Matt and the others just sat and stared at each other, stunned for a moment, before continuing their conversation. It was just another night at the Lizzie Borden Bed & Breakfast.

Weird Pictures in the Sitting Room

I've only been involved in two actual séances in my life, and both were at Lizzie's. Liz Nowicki conducts them for a small fee for guests of the house, and I've been allowed to sit in on them. Being skeptical of the process, I also videotaped them for posterity.

We held one of these séances in the sitting room where Andrew Borden was murdered. As with the rest of the house, the room looks remarkably like

Andrew Borden was found in the sitting room, a victim of ten blows to the head with an ax. *Courtesy of Stefani Koorey.*

it did in 1892, a testament to the restoration work Lee-ann and Donald have done over the years.

During this séance, I was videotaping when someone noticed that my T-shirt was lifting up over my stomach. At first she thought it was just because my arms were holding the camera, but she could see that even as my arms remained steady (I like to think of myself as a more than adequate cameraman, so I know my shot was true) my shirt continued to lift. Someone else snapped a picture of it, and it shows streaks of a mysterious orange light right over the part of my shirt that was being lifted.

That's not the only weird photo that has come out of the sitting room, either. Whenever we bring anyone there for the first time, they've got to stop for the "photo op" in the parlor. A small hatchet is in a woodpile in the kitchen, and the women usually want to swing the hatchet while a man pretends to nap on the couch, in a re-creation of Andrew's murder. Yet every

The sitting room as it looks today. With Luminal and a black light, traces of Mr. Borden's blood can still be seen under the floorboards in the basement.

time, the pictures come out with weird anomalies, including a complete vanishing of the ax itself while in motion—even when the shutter speed is set very high, which it should be for fast-motion capture. Even professional photographers have been baffled by this phenomenon.

The Clock that Stopped

In the sitting room, there is a mantel clock with a very loud tick to it. When the house is deathly silent, you can hear the tick all the way up on the third floor. It is a beautiful decorative piece, but if I had to sleep there, I'd probably end up going downstairs and smashing the thing!

One particular night, we had been investigating for about eight hours and everyone was getting pretty loopy, so we decided to take a break. I sat on the floor of the sitting room with a handful of other people, and we decided to see if we could get the spirits to slow down the clock's tick. Amazingly, within a few minutes it happened—to the point where the clock stopped ticking completely. Then, after a few seconds, it began ticking back furiously in an effort to catch up, before finally returning to normal.

The Noises Upstairs

One of the best parts about the access we have to the Lizzie Borden Bed & Breakfast is the ability to be the only ones there during the off-season. Often, we'll go there to record paranormal television shows, on-site episodes of our radio show or just to investigate with the bare minimum of people around. Jeff Belanger wrote about one incident that happened under those circumstances in the introduction to this book, but it's not the only time we've heard noises like that.

Once, Matt Moniz, a few others and I were seated at the dining room table when upstairs, we could clearly hear the sound of a baby crying. Thoroughly creeped out and knowing nobody else was up there, we tried to ignore it. When we later went to the second floor to continue our investigation, we heard the sound of a woman singing on the third floor.

People often report hearing a loud thump every so often on the third floor. This was also featured on the episode of *Ghost Hunters*, where investigators Donna LaCroix and Andy Andrews heard it while in the Knowlton room. We had the opportunity to investigate the house with Donna on a separate occasion, and we were able to tie what she heard into the reports of those who stay in the Andrew Jennings room right next door—the sound is produced by the heavy foot pedal of the old-fashioned sewing machine slamming to the floor. The question is what slammed it?

One of the scariest sounds we've heard there came one night when we were conducting an EVP session in the Knowlton room. There were about six people in the room, all positioned close to the bed, when we heard a loud and angry-sounding growl coming from the corner, a low guttural sound that we instantly knew was not human. However, when we went to play it back, it didn't show up on any of our recordings.

Shadows of Something Sinister

On August 4, 2009, Matt Moniz and I just happened to be in Fall River on other business on the anniversary of the murders, so we decided to stop in to Lizzie's and say hello to Lee-ann and a number of friends who were there that night. We met a pair of teenagers from out of state who were staying at the house and wanted to know more about the paranormal activity there. We agreed to take them into the basement for a little while and show them how to conduct an investigation, thinking nothing would really come of it.

As usual, when it comes to predicting the activity at the Borden house, we were wrong.

The basement is perhaps the most interesting part of the entire house. It's not part of the daily tour, and it is mostly used for storage, laundry and paranormal investigation. While the activity isn't always as prevalent as it is elsewhere in the house, when something happens in the basement, it's usually something worth noting.

Since we hadn't exactly planned on an investigation, Moniz and I didn't have any of our equipment with us. The two teens just had a video camera and a digital camera. We shut the lights off and began the investigation.

Not long after we began, I started calling out for whatever spirit lives in the basement to come out and show itself. I'm usually quite forceful with this particular entity, for reasons we'll get into in a bit. While I'm going through my whole song-and-dance routine in an effort to get it to come out and play, one of the teens simply asked aloud, "Um, what's that over there?"

Across the basement was a dark human form standing there and staring at us. Blacker than the darkness that surrounded it, we could clearly make out a shadow person, a type of paranormal phenomena that has gained ground in recent years. Not quite a ghost, it is an intelligent entity nonetheless. It watched us for a split second and then bolted.

We were able to follow its movements throughout the basement for a few minutes. The basement is set up as four different rooms, separated mostly by fieldstone. Matt Moniz and I attempted to trap it in the middle room, but when we thought we did so, it simply vanished.

So What Exactly Is Going On?

As I said at the start of this chapter, I'm not going to try to solve the greatest unsolved crime of the last 150 years (with apologies to D.B. Cooper, of course). As an investigator, my job is to document and come up with a hypothesis regarding the activity in the house. In my opinion, the murders are not the cause of the paranormal activity at 92 Second Street—they're just a consequence.

Whatever is in that house predates the Bordens living there. It's what drove a man running from the police into the basement of the house in an attempt to hide, only to be shot dead when they found him. It's what drove the relative next door to throw her own children down a well and then take her own life. It's what drove the escalating tensions between the Bordens themselves, and it all but put the ax in the hands of whoever brought it down on Andrew and Abby.

As we learned in the first part of this book, the Native Americans thought there were spirits in this area long before King Philip's War turned the entire SouthCoast into one mass Indian burial ground. Whatever those spirits may be, they have a history of influencing evil. In the grand scheme of things, Lizzie Borden is not that far removed from Carl Drew and James Kater, or from John Alderman or the abusive orderlies of the Lakeville San. Heck, it's probably only a few degrees of separation from that bunch to the Pukwudgies. When something wicked this way comes, it usually sticks around and has no problems finding minions to do its bidding.

Am I talking about the devil, the very creature those Puritans warned against back when they first came to this land? I don't think so. Whatever this power is, it's beholden to no particular belief system. It's something that is bad just because it is. More negativity is what it lives on, and it finds ways to perpetuate that negativity. Some might refer to it as an elemental, a spirit that was never corporeal and essentially exists solely as a construct.

In discussing its influence on this particular case, look at it like this: You're a spirit that has reigned over this particular spot for millennia. You feed on the negative. Along comes this family, the Bordens, who are already at odds with one another. They fight about money; they fight about position; and they fight because sometimes that's just what happens when you spend too long living with the same people. Either way it's negative, and it's whetting your appetite. You decide to interject a little and influence the situation a bit, just to see how far you can make it—like someone piling food onto their plate at an all-you-can-eat buffet. Even though you could always just get another plate, you want to see just how high you can stack this particular one. It's almost become sport.

Eventually, the situation results into two brutal murders, and your hunger is satiated for about one hundred or so years. You take a long nap while more loving residents live in the house, but when it is opened to the public and people start mentioning murder again, you awaken. That hunger is rising in your belly. Every day, people are coming in and talking about murder and other terrible acts that may have attributed to it, and paying credence to that negativity feeds you again. You're not getting the one-time plate piled to the ceiling as you did before but a constant stream of nibbles, like a slave feeding grapes to Caesar.

The physical presence of such a creature has been speculated for the past few years. One potential sign, which I have experienced for myself, is the rotting garbage smell that is frequently reported in the basement. Demonic and other negative entities are said to give off such unclean and offensive odors.

There is also the strength of force exhibited when the spirits of the house get physical. While it's possible for formerly human spirits to possess such strength, it's rare. Usually that type of power is held by something much darker.

Many investigators coming in with their paranormal equipment, especially Frank's Box-type devices, feature voices of anger and fear. Christopher Moon, a researcher who has combined Sumption's designs with modifications given to him by Thomas Edison from the Other Side, has pieced together through his use of the Telephone to the Dead a rather interesting back story to this tale, one that involves an incestuous relationship between Lizzie and her father that resulted in pregnancies and subsequent abortions performed in the secrecy of the basement by Dr. Seabury Bowen from across the street, the aborted fetus buried beneath the wash basin that Lizzie may have used to wash herself of the blood had she indeed committed the murders of her father and stepmother.

The incest story has always bubbled just below the surface of this tragedy, even since 1892, but it was often relegated as just one theory. However, it has gained steam in recent years, until Faye Musselman made her shocking revelation on my radio show.

According to Musselman, she spent the past two years developing a friendship with direct descendent of Henry Augustus Gardner, a relative of the Bordens through marriage and patriarch of the family in Swansea that was very close to Emma and, for a time, Lizzie as well. Through this friendship, Musselman found out that this descendent had inherited some of Emma Borden's belongings, including letters. Among those letters was one written by Orrin Gardner, son of Henry Augustus, in which he made reference to Lizzie being sexually abused by Andrew, and that most of the Gardners, and even Emma, knew it was happening.

In fact, Musselman believes tight circles within the Fall River elite may have also known, but that it was just something that wasn't spoken about.

If the sexual abuse was true, it would explain the brutality and "overkill" of the murders—nineteen blows to the head of Abby, and ten to Andrew. The passion that must have been behind the murders clearly goes beyond a business enemy of Andrew's or even an intruder, and it indicates that not only did the assailant know the couple, but they also felt wronged by them. It's possible that it's because Andrew did terrible things to Lizzie, and Abby stood by and let it happen. Lizzie might have put up with it as long as she could or could have done so even longer, but when she found out the property she desired was being given to her stepmother instead, it triggered her murderous rage.

It is all speculation, of course, but plausible—especially if that nasty thing in the basement was pulling the strings. Could it have manipulated Andrew into committing that incest? Could it have whispered into Lizzie's ear and driven her to kill? Or did it even have to?

Musselman doesn't necessarily buy into this theory, but she does have an interesting observation about Lizzie Borden's life that could suggest the influence of something sinister. Before the murders, Lizzie was full of hatred and resentment, living a cold life and desiring something better. There is even a legend that after being bothered by a stray cat that Abby had taken in, Lizzie took it into the basement and chopped its head off with an ax. Yet the Lizzie who emerged after her acquittal was a quiet person who gave generously to those in her life and made numerous sizeable donations to animal shelters and nursed sick animals back to health in her beloved Maplecroft home up on the hill.

Some may suggest that the burden of being a Borden was alleviated, and Lizzie could live freely as herself. Others might say she had a guilty conscience about getting away with murder and sought to live a life that might earn her a spot in heaven despite the crime.

Personally, I think she finally broke free of whatever was controlling her back at 92 Second Street. But when she passed away in 1927, it took her once again and brought her back to that very location, where she is trapped forever with the other tormented spirits that can't escape its grasp.

It's just a theory, of course. But just in case, when you do spend the night at the Lizzie Borden Bed & Breakfast, Lee-ann will be happy to provide you with a nightlight in your room at no extra cost.

EPILOGUE

Two men are in a bar and an argument breaks out. It's about something irrelevant, but in the heat of the moment, one man shoots the other. The man dies, the other goes to jail, and the night becomes part of the lore of the bar. Years pass, and shot glasses begin to move in the quiet of closing time as the bartender is cleaning up. Sometimes a shot is heard that shakes the bar but has no source. The place has become haunted, and if you go into the bar and ask staff members about it, they are more than happy to share their experiences. Just pull up a chair, order a few drinks over the course of the night, and they'll tell you all about it.

That's the way it goes in the paranormal world today. The haunted present is born of the traumatic past, and hauntings exist in little pockets with colorful back stories, and the ghosts can always be held at arm's length because you probably will not see or hear anything. But the story still gives you chills—or maybe it was the drink.

The SouthCoast is not like that. There are spots where you can stay at a haunted bed and breakfast or get some pub grub while you hear stories of creaks and dark figures, but the haunted history of this little section of Massachusetts is something more, something deeper where researchers are left wondering, why? More often they are left pondering what it all means. The ghosts are not easy here. Back story does not give you solid possibility, but it gives you context.

History has made it this way. The SouthCoast has long been an area that is a bit off, even back to the days when Wampanoags sold off tracts of land that were sketchy anyway. The other side is a reality here, held deep in the DNA of its citizens and worn like scars in their memories, like where they were during the blizzard of '78. It's passed down easily alongside stories of Johnny Appleseed and John Henry, as well as Benjamin Church and Lizzie Borden; the truth is always second fiddle to the truth of the idea.

I was speaking with Tim one night at a town meeting in Freetown while doing research for a book. I asked the audience if anyone had heard of a Pukwudgie, a troll-like legend that, at the time, was a bit obscure. More than half the audience raised their hands. These were not people in seats to hear about ghosts and monsters. This was a meeting of the historical society who had come to discuss budgets and upcoming events, and most were easily in their sixties.

The supernatural and the paranormal were just part of the complexion of the people.

The spooks just change their face from time to time. There is more than four hundred years of history in the SouthCoast, plenty of time for phantom carriages to become phantom cars, and story to be replaced by story. It is rare in this country to have so many strong cultures imprint themselves on a place, and each has their experience explained partly by the history already there and partly by their own people's slant. Paranormal investigators and ghost hunters can come by with equipment and technology, taking measurements and gathering evidence, but the ghosts were there long before them and will be around when most have moved on to other interests.

There is no separation from paranormal experience and history in the SouthCoast, and delving into the unusual there is more a study in anthropology than parapsychology. Read the books, visit the websites and watch the documentaries. Maybe even visit the sites; but understand you are only getting part of the story. The other part lies in the heart of the people who live here. Don't be discouraged, though. Go to the center of any of these towns, stand on a street corner or under a tree, and ask the first person you see if they know any good ghost stories. They'll smile, and you'll quickly realize you have just become part of the tale.

Christopher Balzano
Author of *Dark Woods: Cults, Crime and the Paranormal in the Freetown State Forest, Ghosts of the Bridgewater Triangle* and *Picture Yourself Ghost Hunting*

BIBLIOGRAPHY

BOOKS

Balzano, Christopher. *Dark Woods: Cults, Crime and the Paranormal in the Freetown State Forest.* Atglen, PA: Schiffer Books, 2007.

———. *Ghosts of the Bridgewater Triangle.* Atglen, PA: Schiffer Books, 2008.

———. *Picture Yourself Ghost Hunting.* Boston: Course Technology PTR, 2008.

Belanger, Jeff. *Picture Yourself Legend Tripping.* Boston: Course Technology PTR, 2010.

———. *Weird Massachusetts.* Toronto, ON: Sterling Publishing, 2008.

DeMello, Thomas, and Thomas Nickerson. *Our Demons, Our Forefathers: Ghostly Encounters in a Sleepy New England Town.* N.p.: AuthorHouse, 2006.

Kent, David. *The Lizzie Borden Sourcebook.* Boston: Branden Books, 1992.

Lovell, Daisy. *Glimpses of Early Wareham.* Wareham, MA: Wareham Historical Society, 1970.

Rehak, David. *Did Lizzie Borden 'Axe' For It?* N.p.: Angel Dust Publishing, 2008.

Rider, Raymond A. *Life and Times in Wareham over 200 Years 1739–1939.* Wareham, MA: Wareham Historical Society, 1989.

Robinson, Charles Turek. The *New England Ghost Files.* North Attleborough MA: Covered Bridge Press, 1994.

PERIODICALS AND PAPERS

Albernaz, Ami. "Japanese Men, Spinner Publications Collaborate on Manjiro Nakahama Story." *Standard-Times*, May 25, 2003.

Aubut, Rebecca. "Fact or Fiction? The Search for the Truth Behind Fairhaven's Haunted Library." October 25, 2005. Southcoast247.com, http://www.southcoast247.com.

Barnes, Jennette. "313-year-old Middleboro Tavern Closes Abruptly." *Standard-Times*, January 11, 2004.

———. "Captive Memories: Author Recalls Childhood as Tuberculosis Patient at Lakeville State Hospital." *Standard-Times*, June 22, 2004.

Boston Daily Globe. "Glen Charlie." December 3, 1885.

Guille, Sarah, and Robert Lovinger. "VIP, RIP: A Brief Tour of the Final Resting Places of Some Famous, Infamous and Just Plain Interesting People of SouthCoast's Past." *Standard-Times*, May 30, 1999.

Massachusetts Historical Commission. *Massachusetts Historical Commission Reconnaissance Survey Town Report: WAREHAM*. Report. Southeast Massachusetts, 1981.

Some Account of the Vampires of Onset, Past and Present. Boston: Press of S. Woodbury and Company, 1892.

WEBSITES

American Heritage. http://www.americanheritage.com/articles/magazine/ah/1992/4/1992_4_66.shtml.

Biographical Sketch of John Gage. http://files.usgwarchives.org/il/montgomery/bios/johngage.txt.

A Chronological History of New Bedford. http://www.newbedford.com/chrono.html.

Fairhaven, Massachusetts. http://www.fairhaven.net

Fort Phoenix, Fairhaven, Massachusetts. http://fort-phoenix.blogspot.com.

Friends of Historic Preservation, Freetown, Massachusetts. http://www.assonetriver.com/preservation.

Ghostvillage. http://www.ghostvillage.com.

Greenville Paranormal Reasearch. http://www.greenvilleparanormal.com.

Haunted Lakeville. http://www.hauntedlakeville.com.

Haunted Places Index-Massachusetts. http://www.theshadowlands.net/places/Massachusetts.

The Kinsale Inn. http://www.kinsaleinn.com.

Lizzie Andrew Borden Virtual Museum and Library. http://www.lizzieandrewborden.com.

Lizzie Borden Bed & Breakfast. http://www.lizzie-borden.com.

Massachusetts Paranormal Crossroads. http://www.masscrossroads.com.

Recollecting Namasket. http://nemasket.blogspot.com/2010/07/lakeville-state-sanatorium-design.html.

RideAccidents.com. http://www.rideaccidents.com.

Tattered Fabric. http://phayemuss.wordpress.com.

Town of Dartmouth, Massachusetts. http://town.dartmouth.ma.us/Pages/DartmouthMA_Webdocs/darthistory.

Town of Fairhaven, Massachusetts. http://www.fairhaven-ma.gov.

Town of Lakeville, Massachusetts. http://www.lakevillema.org.

Town of Marion, Massachusetts. http://www.marionma.gov/Pages/index.

Town of Mattapoisett, Massachusetts. http://www.mattapoisett.net.

Town of Rochester, Massachusetts. http://www.townofrochestermass.com.

Town of Wareham, Massachusetts. http://www.wareham.ma.us.

The Wamsutta Club Online. http://www.wamsuttaclub.net.

Westport (Massachusetts) History. http://westporthistory.com.

ABOUT THE AUTHOR

Tim Weisberg is the host of *Spooky Southcoast*, one of the world's most popular radio programs dealing with the subject of the paranormal. He's also been featured in publications such as *FATE Magazine*, *SoCo Magazine* and *SouthCoast Insider* and on television on the History Channel, Discovery Channel, *30 Odd Minutes* and LIVING TV in the UK. A sportswriter by trade, Tim covers the Boston Celtics and the New England Patriots for the *Standard-Times* of New Bedford, Massachusetts. He can be reached via email at tim@spookysouthcoast.com.

Visit us at
www.historypress.net